EASY ON THE GREASE

David James Lavisher was born in 1943 in Moorside and grew up in the village. His teenage years were spent sampling the somewhat dubious delights to be found in and around Oldham, in its decadent and exciting heyday of the late 1950s to the early 1960s (wherein lies this story). Other leisure time in his youth was taken up playing football in Oldham's Amateur Football Leagues and he was a motorcyclist for a few years until he was fed up with being wet through most of the time.

For the bulk of his adult life, David was employed by Oldham M.B.C., working in the Environmental Health Department – a job that he enjoyed.

For the past 28 years he has written poetry with some success. In the late 1970s and early 1980s his poems were published regularly in *Lancashire Life* magazine, the *Oldham Weekend Chronicle* – often, the *Huddersfield Examiner* – intermittently since then. Many others appeared in national magazines and various anthologies.

He has been a prizewinner in poetry competitions over the years – the most recent being in the Lancashire Authors' Association – of which he is a member – winning their 'Poetry in Standard English 2001' competition and was pleased to win their 'Writer of the Year Award 2001'.

David attended the Blue Coat School in Oldham and is a member of the ex-pupils' Old Blues Association. He lives in Slaithwaite, West Yorkshire, with his wife Sylvia. They like to travel abroad, visiting friends in America and driving round Europe enjoying historical cities and different cultures. At home, he writes and does a spot of fishing when time permits. He has another book in progress – a fiction novel in its early stages.

Previous books:

Poems for Pleasure. Self-published in 1994.

A Moorside Lad – Growing up and having fun 1948–1955 published 2002 by Jade Publishing Limited.

Easy on the Grease

The Rock and Roll years
in a Northern town

Best Wishes

david lavisher

David J. Lavisher

JADE

Jade Publishing Limited

5 Leefields Close, Uppermill, Oldham, Lancashire OL3 6LA

This first impression published by Jade Publishing Limited 2004.

ISBN 1–900734–32–X Easy on the Grease – The Rock and Roll years in
                                          a Northern town.

Printed in Great Britain

Typeset by Jade Publishing Limited, Oldham, Lancashire OL3 6LA

British Library Cataloguing in Publication Data
Lavisher, David James
Easy on the Grease – The Rock and Roll years in a northern town
1. Lavisher, David James – Childhood and youth 2. Oldham (England) –
Biography 3. Oldham (England) – Social life and customs
4. Saddleworth (England) – Social life and customs
I. Title
942.7'393'085'092

ISBN 1–900734–32–X

This book is dedicated
to Sylvia

CONTENTS

ILLUSTRATIONS

There are ten pictures between pages 92 and 93. All copyrights are acknowledged and permission was sought, and granted, to reproduce the pictures shown in this work.

Anyone wishing to contact David Lavisher may do so through his email address: castleshaw@aol.com. or view his website: www.hometown.aol.co.uk/dovestones/davidlavisher.html.

All orders for copies of the book should be addressed to Jade Publishing Limited, 5, Leefields Close, Uppermill, Oldham, Lancashire, OL3 6LA.

The cover by Baxter-Cox Design.

COPYRIGHT ACKNOWLEDGEMENTS

Acknowledgements

I would like to thank my wife Sylvia for her help; particularly when I've been a damn disagreeable nuisance.

Jo Qualters for her early rooting out of my more obvious deviations from the theme.

Brian Prescott (Jade Publishing Limited) for his advice and friendship.

Pamela Daniels (Editor) for allowing a little licence with the text.

The *Oldham Evening Chronicle* for photographs.

The people below who have kindly agreed to let me put names to incidents or accounts.

Dave Royle	George Richards
Lawrie Turner	Peter Tildsley
John Buckley	Alan Tunnicliffe
Winston Howes	Martin Warburton
John Mahoney	Tony Whitehead
Bob Marsden	Jack Whitehead
Stuart Radcliffe	

There are incidents concerning people that I have been unable to contact. In those cases, where I have thought it necessary, I have used fictitious names or given them names that they would not normally answer to.

David J. Lavisher
October, 2004

FOREWORD

Easy On The Grease is the review of a journey back to youth in the late 1950s, early 1960s. It came about by my lowering a bucket into the well of my early life to see what came up when I cranked the winding handle. The capital letter 'I' appears more often than it should, however my being the narrator means there is no way around that. The account is about the roller-coaster life of a teenager operating in the town of Oldham towards the end of the Rock and Roll era and later moving on to the relatively quieter environs of Saddleworth. Music and girls formed the basis for existence; jukeboxes and record players met that need in the first instance and visits to the local dancehalls in the latter. In my time, the Savoy Dancehall (which is now The Candlelight Club) the cinemas and public houses were the main town-centre evening attractions. The town was alive, bursting at the seams with noise and bustle and lads in their mid/late teens – most with more lip than an auctioneer – ran between the town's public houses as if their landlords had been ordered to introduce rationing. Girls spending time in town stood by and watched them doing it – no doubt with some amusement. In reality our lives would be like a slender thread passing through the principle functions of the town. However, we didn't know that at the time. Oldham was an artistically austere town and thrived upon the work ethic; it was a tough place to spend time and hadn't yet learned how to smile – if it ever has. At that time in our lives, we thought we were gods – untouchable. If you had a need to touch us, your first priority was to catch us.

The second half of the book takes on a different aspect and moves to Saddleworth, which was not part of Oldham, being an outpost of the West Riding of Yorkshire. However much some people decry the old saying about the grass being greener on the far side of the hill, occasionally the maxim holds true. There is a lot more grass in Saddleworth than in Oldham town centre for a start.

I was born in the Pennine village of Moorside, Oldham, Lancashire, approximately one mile short of the Yorkshire boundary and may not be the person best qualified to carry out the summary of events that happened in Saddleworth. However there is no requirement to have been baptised at St. Thomas' Church, Friarmere,

Delph, or any other place of worship in Saddleworth, to speak happily or frankly about a place that I have known, lived in and liked for many years. The only excuse that I can offer for my impudence is that I have spent half my life in the district one way or another. With very few exceptions my time in the green hills and cool valleys has been a pleasurable experience. The period seems to have been a hiccough in Saddleworth history before the place settled down, waiting – in my view – to be exploited.

The degree of youthful turbulence within the book is reasonable and there is a decent amount of irreverence sprinkled around. Those who have never sailed close to the wind or wanted to for that matter, can share some of our younger years without having to bear the pain that was sometimes involved. You can have my times; I'm not peevish that way. If you want my money, we'll have to negotiate. I have tried to write the piece as a lightly humorous, whimsical look back in time and it is not intended as a factual account.

I hope that it will be read with those caveats in mind.

David J. Lavisher
August, 2004

1

Wake up, little Susie, wake up.
Wake up, little Susie, wake up.
We've both been sound asleep,
Wake up little Susie and weep,
The movie's over, it's four o'clock and we're in trouble deep.
Wake up, little Su-u-sie,
Wake up, little Susie.
We godda go home.

The year was 1958. The Everly Brothers were visiting Lawrie's older sisters in their front room as I was leaving his house. Don and Phil Everly visited most young ladies of the previous generation to mine, along with Eddie Cochran, Gene Vincent, Freddie Cannon, Duane Eddy, Don Gibson, Johnnie Burnett, Don Lang and The Kalin Twins. The period was a rich time for Rock and Roll music; most of the crooners and dance bands of the previous era were heading for retirement, the clubs or the dole queue. I could hear the popular duo, their voices wailing out of a half-open front room window, from the pavement outside our house, which was situated directly across the street from Lawrie's.

Mind you, prior to that and equally to my liking, Elvis had been asking the girls for *A Bigga Bigga Bigga Hunk A Love* in his usual unsophisticated fashion – meaning that half the time I couldn't tell one word from the next. Sometimes, when we were all together and walking down the road feeling *synchronized*, we enjoying ten minutes of communal singing to some Elvis song or other. Mr. Presley's songs were often accredited with words that he hadn't actually uttered or probably hadn't even thought about. Some words bore little resemblance to the ones originally written and other interpretations were passed over with a loud intake of breath and repetitious vowel sounds. Rewarding listening I'm sure, for the tone deaf, devotees of *The Chipmunks* and those of an excessively tolerant nature.

Lawrie, along with Terry and Bob, formed the nucleus of our group and I considered him to be my mate. There were a couple of other lads who were unable or didn't want to be with the group all the time. We were four, 15-year-old lads who hadn't really got started on youth's bequeathed battles against quiet music, moderate clothing, spots, cash-free pockets and the 11 o'clock curfew. All fairly tall with recently arrived sideburns, we had a greatly exaggerated opinion of our own importance and a self-destruct button planted firmly in the middle of our over-active imaginations. Looking back and with more than a grain of truth, our wooden front gate probably knew more about the workings of the outside world than we did.

The time was early Saturday afternoon and it was a warm sunny day. We were all going into town to see if we could find any girls who looked as if they were in need of a bit of impressing. The trip had become a regular thing of late and really we would be going to buy denim jeans or new shoes, "clobber" as it was known, but if the opportunity arose to impress a few …

As I stepped automatically over the ill-fitting grid cover in the middle of the concrete footpath bisecting the front garden of our house, a cool breeze blew open my denim jacket, pushing against the obligatory white tee shirt. Patting breeze-blown hair down with the palm of my hand and remembering to set my face in its hood-eyed scowl, I waited a few seconds before entering our kitchen door, which was situated down the side wall of our house, towards the rear.

Our house was a 1930s-built, red brick, three bedroom, semi-detached property belonging to Oldham Council Housing Department and numbered 20 Strinesdale Close (now Hayfield Close) in the village of Moorside, Oldham. The house was better than any we had lived in previously, if only for the fact that it had a bathroom, a separate toilet and a further one downstairs next to the back door. The downstairs toilet was only of any use if you were taken short. Should someone be holding a lengthy conversation at the door and you were in occupancy, you could be in there for a long time. (The toilet at the other house had been thirty yards away across a flat cobbled farmyard. In the bitter winters of the late 1940s, the yard often transformed itself into two, five-foot-high snowdrifts and a patch of ice the size of Lake Michigan.) The current house had gardens back and front, the rear one being accessible by a balcony running along the side and round the rear of the house and then split-level steps leading down. If you were prone to attacks of vertigo, it wasn't wise to look over the balcony wall at the garden, some fourteen to sixteen feet below. The houses in 'The Close', with the exception of the three across the top, were built into a hillside. The view from the balconies of some of the even-numbered ones gave an unrestricted outlook onto the houses and mills in the village of Waterhead some two miles distant across grazing meadows and two reservoirs. (Waterhead must have incorporated Germany within its boundaries at some time or other. I'd be about nine years old and asked a lad who was doing his stint of National Service, where the Germans lived. 'Over there', he replied, pointing towards Waterhead and that was good enough for me). Our house had a separate coal place with a washhouse attached; the latter became a small workshop for my father, housing tools and bits of motorbike engines and my Dad a lot of the time. My father only needed to hear an unusual comment from his motorbike's engine and the bike was soon stripped down into tiny pieces. In this pleasurable pursuit he was ably assisted by a lad of my age named Robert, who lived a couple of streets away. Bob was the eldest in a large brood of children and was my father's unpaid, weekend apprentice. Come rain or shine, by ten o'clock in the morning, the lad was up to his elbows in nuts and bolts. We had no use for the washhouse in its intended form because we owned a huge top-loading *Ada* washing machine which half filled our kitchen. It was quite tall, therefore any items that required washing could only be put into it by standing on a chair, or trying a number of unorthodox basketball shots. The *Ada* had power rollers for squeezing water out of bedding or garments and crushed into powder any clothes buttons unlucky enough to pass between them. The machine was temperamental and my father spent a fair bit of his time playing about with it. The only other appliance in the kitchen was an electric cooker, supplied by the Housing Department and manufactured by a company named *Revo*. For culinary purposes it had one oblong hot plate that doubled underneath as a grill, two ring plates and a small oven. Its other purpose was to keep our cat Ginger warm while he ate his food underneath it. A thing of style and beauty it wasn't. Well, it might have been to Salvador Dali or those other unusual portrayers of art. The oven was ignorant of the fact that it had a dial for thermostatic control to assist with cooking lighter-textured food such as sponge cakes. When it had reached maximum heat and readiness and was glowing triumphantly, the cooker ticked ominously, its heat peeling back the sticky-backed imitation-tile plastic lining in the recess, which housed it. The thing was enamelled in biliously flecked white on grey and sat on four twelve-inch-high legs from which it spent most of its time staring nastily at the *Ada* washing machine. The appliance would make perfect toast for our

3

mother but always burned my slices of bread until they were of the same consistency as our cork tablemats. I recall one Christmas when I was given a very large turkey by whichever firm I was working with at the time. I've mentioned that the oven was on the small side. Our mother tried all ways to get the turkey to fit inside it. Eventually, after much muscle flexing by the bird and a considerable amount of grunting from our mother, the turkey was inserted from lower corner to upper opposite corner in a fairly deep oven tray. The oven being electrically powered meant that most of the heat came through its side walls; consequently the Parson's Nose of the turkey looked considerably more distressed than your average parson's nose. However much it tried, the oven never outwitted our mother who produced some pretty good meals from within its searing innards.

Conway Twitty had ousted the Everly Brothers from Lawrie's front room so I waited a further minute or two, thinking that I'd listen to his song. He was reaching down into his diaphragm for the deep notes that began his current hit song *Only Makebelieve*

> *Peoble see us everywhere, they thenk you really care,*
> *Bud mahself ah caint deceive, ah know it's only makebe-lieve.*
> *Mah one an' only prayer, is that some day...*

I was standing by the back door and busying myself trying to beat Mr. Twitty to the top note at the end of the first verse when I heard a deep rumbling voice, one that I wouldn't ordinarily expect to hear issuing from the depths of our living room. Conway wasn't to be denied his airspace and carried on with his delusions, while my voice detector tried its best to put a face to the unfamiliar voice issuing from the depths of our house. The singer's voice started to rise, as he got fairly upset about his unrequited love. At the peak of his distress, his voice was well up in the tone of scale and as I walked through the door, it began following me into the kitchen. I soon put it out of its misery by banging the door shut, an act that often incurred the wrath of someone with seniority in our family rankings and always gave our china crockery an attack of noisy jitters. I had another go at placing the voice, screwing my face up in what I hope passed for a thoughtful expression. Nope, didn't know the owner of the voice – I hadn't a clue.

'Now then young man', he said, occupying my mother's fireside chair, trying to hold a cup of tea on its saucer and balance his helmet on his knees at the same time.

'What've you been up to in the village?'

This was the second time I had given P.C. William Webster (known as Bill in his absence) cause to avail himself of a cup of my mother's Horniman's tea. The first time had occurred some years earlier when as children a few of us decided to make our twenty-foot -high bonfire into a thirty-foot-high one by removing some wooden fencing belonging to Holroyd's the farming family at Little End Farm, Strinesdale. When I was a youngster, anything made from wood got itself onto the list of 'desirable combustibles' in late October/early November. Were you a person reduced to using wooden crutches or a walking stick it wasn't wise to leave them lying around unattended at that time of year.

'Up to no good last night in The Villas, were you?', he asked again.

The Villas was the exclusive part of our village. They were and are large expensive houses, running up both sides of Ripponden Road near the Waggon and Horses pub, ending where the road opens out into countryside, half a mile short of the Yorkshire boundary. P.C. Webster was referring to our recent operations concerning the law, taking it into our own hands and thoroughly breaking it.

The previous evening, at around seven thirty – a bright midsummer's night it was too – in full view of everyone from Birmingham to Newcastle, five of us had left the aforementioned Waggon and Horses pub after drinking two pints each of Wilson's Mild beer. In a few moments of spontaneous, drink-influenced lunacy, while thinking we hadn't been observed, we'd broken some ornamental gatepost copings and a couple of large windows belonging to the big houses nearby. To be more precise, the houses were numbered 799 and 803 Ripponden Road. (Throwing stuff must be hereditary in our family, my father was always throwing my sharpened penknives away and Grandfather spent a lot of his time being thrown out of the house when he had been drinking). We were later told that a chap in one of the houses was looking out of his front room window when a missile arrived to render it opaque. He can't have been thrilled when that happened, especially if he was wearing glasses, he wouldn't immediately know which item had shattered.

He was the man on the spot, so to speak and quickly identified the backs of our rapidly vanishing heads. We were supposed to be following in the tradition of youth and occasionally taking a bite from the trouble-apple as we trod the path to adult enlightenment. Being greedy types, we ate the apple at one go – core and all. It was to be the last time that I would let my mind be completely taken over by anything other than sleep and anaesthesia.

Unprepared as I was to see a large lump of the local constabulary occupying half of our living room, I managed to grunt something unintelligible in answer to his question which was more of a statement I suppose. From then onwards it was a matter of him speaking and me not. Our living room was a smallish affair with a large, square, patterned carpet, which fell a foot or so short of the skirting boards. The exposed floorboards were teak-stained and then varnished over. The rest of the room was taken up by two wooden-armed fireside chairs, one four-foot-square extendible dining table and four matching chairs, one large old-fashioned sideboard, one round-topped table with a barley sugar single-twist leg, upon which lived a largish, wooden, Sunray radio. The set had an eight-inch speaker that could be seen through its fabric-covered front when the sun hit certain parts of the room. The radio was content to function correctly during the day but in the evenings it did a lot of crackling and hissing if it was asked to produce sound from a station that it couldn't quite put its finger on.

With my father and Constable Webster comfortably at their ease, there wasn't much room left for me, so I chose to stand in the doorway – just in case it got a bit hot in there. I could see my Dad was less than impressed with the situation. A similar condition was present in our ginger tomcat, which ruled the house from a cardboard box in the connecting passageway between the kitchen and living room. Smart, as he surely was, our cat only responded to two words – "Ginger" and that centuries-old command most beloved of fathers and pet owners, "Geroffmichair". He was a malingerer of the first order, with years of experience in the identification of storm clouds about to gather under the roof of our house. His home significantly reduced the width of the passageway, probably accounting for the state of apprehension that he regularly found himself in. When he was about half grown it wasn't unusual to see him peering over the top of his box, ears laid back, looking as if he was about to receive incoming rounds from a machine-gun.

The constable was a large man; his boots were in proportion to his size and one false step in passing – well, it would have been unfortunate for Ginger. (When I was a child, all policemen were large, carrying a small whistle and a large truncheon. Recently I was passing through Town Square in Oldham and saw the shortest of policemen, with enough webbing festooned about his person to hang all our kitchen utensils on, his belt had more pouches than a mutant kangaroo and he was affecting a wide-armed swagger intended to keep the town's enthusiastic purveyors of mischief separated from the peace loving public).

I'm not sure how we acquired the cat; it's possible that my sister Jean dragged it in when it was a kitten. Throughout his early life Ginger was prone to long bouts of absenteeism and could often be seen gadding about Holroyd's farm across the way, keeping the resident mice on their toes and joining in any feline choral production that the farm cats put on. When he eventually decided that he preferred the Bed and Breakfast arrangements in our house, he graduated from the cardboard box to a sumptuous mortgage-free cat basket. My father, not into property buying at the time, although he and our mother were well on their way to a deposit for one, was heard to mutter, 'Ah, never mind about the cost, buy him one.' Not having heard that phrase spoken by him before, I wondered if he had coined a new expression for the world to enjoy.

P.C. Webster swung his pale blue eyes, chubby cheeks and blond moustache in my direction when the silence had reached well into the discomfort zone. Pinning me against the end of our sideboard with his unblinking gaze, he carried on growling pleasantries in between taking sips of his tea. I remember switching off after a while and just picking out key words like "court", "fines" and "good hiding" in the ensuing fifteen minutes or so.

'How old are you now David, fifteen is it?' Bill knew how many times a week I had a wash, never mind how old I was.

'Young people have a limited responsibility to be a nuisance,' he said, looking at me as if he was addressing a mobster.

Straightening up at this point in his monologue, he leaned forward, moustache bristling, and took a long draw of his tea.

'But not on my patch' he said, after a moment's pause and a loud 'Tah' of tea-drinker's appreciation.

He looked across the room at my father, who nodded sagely.

'I'll have to do something about it, Joe.' Bill said.

My father nodded sagely again.

Father was a great believer in "doing something about it". When he was eighteen, he and his mate Conny Costello were of a mind to give Adolph Hitler a going-over – long before the army got round to inviting them to join its ranks – and they joined up. Another case in point occurred when I was about seven years old. A youth twice my age, who regularly visited someone nearby, was in the habit of punching me around the head, using that as his means for relieving the boredom. One day he overdid it a bit and painted the middle of my face a smeary red colour. When my messy face presented itself in our kitchen for inspection and I'd explained the circumstances that had brought it about, my father was a bit miffed. He walked to the pantry where my playing-out clogs were kept and very quickly fitted them to my feet; the clogs were fastened by a snap-on clip and had a shiny, inch wide metal strip across the toe section. Walking at a pace that ensured I had very little contact with the ground, we approached the lad outside his grandmother's (he looked very big from where I was standing) and my father said to me,

'Kick him, go on, kick him hard, in the shins.'

I didn't think that was a very good idea.

Seeing my reluctance, my father spoke again,

'Kick him or I'll belt you one.'

You know how it is, whichever way it goes you lose. So I gave the lad a woofter on the shin and then stood back two paces to see what happened next. The lad was beautifully balanced as he hopped up and down the road holding his leg as if it was about to fall off. We departed the scene in triumph – well, my father did. I had to be very careful when I stuck my nose out of the door for quite a while afterwards. "Doing something about it" can be worrisome at times.

As an aside to the general thread of the story, my father was not well disposed towards acts of public violence and had a grievous dislike for guns of any type when he came home from the Second World War. When I was ten years old or so, using our balcony wall for the purpose, he furiously reduced to fire kindling and slivers of metal, a replica rifle with the original stock and a length of half-inch tubing, which acted as the gun barrel. I remember thinking, as I covered my head in an attempt to dodge the shrapnel, that his actions were fine by me, except the rifle wasn't mine. Filling an old bucket with the shattered bits of rifle, I quietly placed them on Wally Gartside's back doorstep, (he being the lad that had loaned it to me) and legged it home. I didn't catch the bus outside their house for a while after that, he had an older brother of unregulated temperament. Curiously, father didn't resist when I was fourteen years old and his friend from work offered to teach me to shoot with a rifle. My father and Roy (who lived in Cobden Street at Waterhead) both worked in the blacksmith's shop at Seddon Diesel (later to become Seddon Atkinson) at Heyside. Roy was a great bear of a man and as is often the case, was as pleasant a guy as you could wish to meet – and he could shoot. He had a few rifles mounted on a gun rack above the fireplace in the family home, a .22 rifle that fired bullets, a .303 army issue rifle and a double-barrelled shotgun. (In those days people didn't go round shooting shopkeepers or holding up banks – not in Moorside or Waterhead they didn't anyway). The hillsides in the old quarry at High Moor, Scouthead must have had more bullets in them than Kynoch manufactured in a year's production. No S.W.A.T. teams turned up to investigate the gunfire.

Picking up the thread again. Deep in P.C Webster's eyes, I thought I could see the reflection of iron bars and hear cell doors clanging shut – although it was probably my mother reshaping the cooking pans in the kitchen sink, a common way for her to vent her ire at a situation she wasn't pleased with. When the inquisition was over and Bill had put his helmet on – after a second cup of tea of course – he arose from the chair, having to stoop almost double to pass under the doorframe and get back into the kitchen. I don't know what Ginger thought Bill was about to do as he loomed over his abode but it must have been something that he considered to be life threatening because he set off for the rear exit as if Paddy the dog from next door was after him. A sharp flurry of confused activity surrounded the door as bodies rushed forward to open it before Ginger could throw a feline tantrum and attack something dear to our mother. Objects available to him, if I remember correctly, were a cooked chicken cooling on the cold pantry shelf, four rows of newly-washed bedding hanging in long folds from the overhead drying rack, a red jelly trying to set itself next to a large plate full of homemade cakes, both standing on the worktop of the kitchen cupboards. If he didn't fancy any of those, Ginger had the kitchen curtains to go at – which to the best of my knowledge had never met each other in all the time they had been hung on the curtain rail. After the scrimmage had disentangled itself, Ginger was off like a startled whippet. I think he took a bit of leave that he was overdue and stayed on the farm for a couple of days after that.

A short time later I recounted the interview with Bill to the other participants in our crime and some of them said that during that morning they had listened in silence to a similar version. Except for the lad whose mother threw a fit and anything else of minor value that she could lay her hands on, before asking the quickly emptying room,

'What will the neighbours think?' All my mates lived nearby: Lawrie across the road, Terry at the top of the street and Bob farther along Roebuck Lane not far from the Roebuck Inn on High Moor. John, who drifted away from the group when we started going into town regularly, was a couple of years older than us and lived on the next street. Jack, the younger of the two lads who lived next door to us had been a member of our group and was one year younger than us, which meant that we could go carousing while he, not yet working, couldn't. I can't recall when Roger joined us on a regular basis – it was later on anyway. After a bit of kerb-kicking and a lot of injured-innocence posturing, we turned like a group of pointer dogs in the direction of town, knowing that our time to move on for future entertainment had arrived. (I ignored what I thought was a faint round of applause from the occupants of the village graveyard, as we passed it on the way to Roger's house). In our imaginations we could hear the town's pleasure establishments restocking their jukeboxes with records in anticipation of our arrival. In the very near future, jukebox music was to follow us around all the time. Loud and brash, it would be a constant in our young lives.

Family involvement from that time onwards was restricted to, 'I'm goin' out now.' 'What's for tea mum?' 'Where's mi clean jeans?' and 'Can you lend me a ten bob note while weekend?'

I remember my father saying around that time, that money and any remnants of intelligence that remained with me from school would soon be departing, the latter heading in a southerly direction. He was correct. Not long after his prophecy, youthful exuberance, loud voices and continual bursts of bounding energy left the field of play to be substituted by their brother affectations, cool, swagger and vanity (solicitors for recalcitrant youth).

How swift and easy is the transition from childhood innocence to adult corruption. It was great!

A few weeks elapsed before the summons arrived from the Magistrates Court in Oldham, a venue that we all attended. People with briefcases and others with sheaves of paper continually asked our names and dozens of policemen wandered around the place while we waited our turn to be reprimanded. I don't know about anyone else, but when I see a policeman these days I feel as if I should take him home for an hour or two because I might not see another one for a while. As the proceedings got under way we were obliged to stand in a line on the floor of the court, much like swallows on a telephone line, while a chap – the one who wasn't on our side – read out a list of our indiscretions. The list seemed interminable. One of the two ladies – along with the man – who made up the bench, looked at us in a frowning, severe manner when the chap had finished his ruminations and sat down. There was a lot of um-ing and ah-ing between the three of them, accompanied by the occasional look in our direction, presumably to see if we were still there.

'What have you got to say for yourselves?' the nice, homely-looking lady on the right-hand side of the bench asked.

For a bunch of lads who couldn't keep their mouths shut while going about their normal business, a reply to that perfectly reasonable question wasn't about to reveal itself. In my case, the answer would have been somewhere between a stammering mumble and a need to go to the toilet. I managed to suppress both outpourings and said nothing. Meanwhile the other lads occupied themselves with some youthful foot shuffling and intermittent displays of discomfort. Short of a pointed gun, a response of any kind on that side of Christmas wasn't going to be forthcoming. Some of our parents had hired a solicitor, who told the magistrates that under normal circumstances we were good, clean living, honest and reliable, hard-working lads – *some* of which was true, bless him. The justice system does seem to thrive on half-truths, fanciful imagination and downright lies; it's all to do with money I suppose, or the making of it by representative bodies. The Clerk to the Court advised the magistrates of the penalties that they could burden us with and after a further period of time in conference, they loaded us up. The lady sitting in the middle of the three decrees, who looked as if she had eaten something sour recently, passed judgment on us. We were fined, made to pay restitution for the damage and later we got an unflattering mention in the *Oldham Evening Chronicle*. Looking around at the contents of the courtroom, the seating, steps, wall panelling, and bench fascia, everything seemed to be dark and wooden including the announcement of our retribution. After a further period of discourse from the magistrates, a large chap with rolled-up shirt sleeves, who wasn't averse to a bit of shoving and pushing when he thought there was more life in us than we were showing, led us away from the court.

A very cheerful policeman took our photographs, each of us in turn holding a black metal plate with white numbers slotted across it, to add to the Borough's collection. His was the first instance that we'd come across, of someone pointing a camera in our direction and saying, 'Don't smile'. A different policeman tried to take our fingerprints; not easy, because some old lag had told us that if we used sandpaper on our finger-ends the ink would only leave blots on the form issued for that purpose and therefore wouldn't be of any use as a means of identification in the future. The policeman delegated to do the fingerprinting spoke in a foreign language to one of his associates across the room; he said something like, 'Cleverlittlebuggers thislot aren'tthijust?'

Those events took place downstairs from the courtrooms, not far from a short corridor with rooms that had iron doors stretching along both sides, something similar in style to the passageways in a French motel. Although the main constabulary was an integral part of Oldham Town Hall and therefore the courts, the public entrance to the Police Station was on Swan Street. The identification procedures for future reference I wouldn't have minded too much, but none of us had any intention of becoming career criminals – I hadn't that's for sure. As I've previously noted, my mother wasn't present when the interview with P.C. Webster was held in our sitting room and she didn't deprive anyone of a seat in the Magistrates Court either, but I'd put money on it with regard to what she was thinking. 'I've reared a prospective murderer, possibly a bank robber, someone who spits out in public, or at the very least one of those ignorant, bad mannered, loudly crunching apple-eaters that get on everyone's nerves.'

Once the dust had died down after the assessment by our elders (the fines etc.), I was in hock to mother for the sum of five pounds and ten shillings. She didn't know she was in this position until she eventually arrived home from work that day.

After a prolonged bout of ignoring me she asked that short but very specific question. 'Well?'

I gave her a quick appraisal of the day's events from a fault-free point of view. She listened while buttering the bread for tea and then said in one burst of breath, 'Serves you right, that'll teach you, get out of my sight, your tea will be ready at six o'clock, don't be late or you'll get none and I want paying back'. The arrangement of words may not be in the right order and there will be some missing; 'ashamed of yourself' and 'you mark my words, my lad', were staples when my mother was of a mind to air her full collection of rebukes.

A woman of direct words was mother – the opportunities for misinterpretation were few.

I was more than a little interested in what my Dad might say when he came in from work. He had a routine when he arrived home; he would walk down the hallway to his side of the wall-mounted coat rack near the front vestibule door and divest himself of 40lbs of motorcycle gear, place his shoes in the broom cupboard under the stairs and go to the kitchen sink to wash his hands.

'How's your day been Mom?' he'd ask (he always did), as mother was going about her business making the tea. Before she could answer, he'd walk into the sitting room opening the evening paper as he went to sit in his fireside chair, first removing Ginger of course who had shared occupancy rights. Mother was equal to his detachment on that occasion and followed him in as far as the doorway to answer his question – like it or not.

Meanwhile he'd asked me the inevitable question, 'How did you go on in court?'

Before I could draw the deep breath that always preceded giving him an account, mother told him how *her* day had been.

Her day of course was my day.

'He says he's been fined and ...'. Many more words than I can recall were spoken at that juncture.

Her information ended with, '... and he'd better pay me back too, or else.'

(I didn't know who 'Else' was, so mother got the money).

The recounting was accompanied by a raised-eyebrow, admonishing stare. The same stare that she gave me a couple of years later when I optimistically told her that the five pounds board and lodgings I handed over each week, should easily pay for my food, clothes, toiletries and bus fares. What was left over should take me on holiday, buy me a car, tax and insure it and put petrol in.

'Don't forget, pay it back or you'll be in big trouble my lad'. There were many levels of trouble in our house. Mother returned to her task in the kitchen in her usual pan-rattling fashion, preparing to put the tea out. For some reason, my mistakes could only be thoroughly aired at meal times – a captive audience I suppose.

My father grunted 'Humph' and I presume searched the newspaper for the retelling by a reliable informant, *i.e.* the *Oldham Evening Chronicle* courts reporter. The story probably appeared in the following day's newspaper, our case not being heard until just before lunchtime.

My sister Jean, who was around nine or ten years of age and liked to be seated first at the dining table for reasons of her own, was taking only a perfunctory interest in the storm. She seemed to be undisturbed by the crisp volleys of words rattling from our mother and carried on swinging her feet to some invisible rhythm. Jean was an affable child most of the time; it took a lot to ruffle her feathers. At times, if Jean's feathers did look a bit ruffled – it was as well to watch out. I usually got an amused sidelong glance across the dining table from "our kid" when I'd erred – which was pretty often. Looking back on it, she always had an inscrutable look about her when I was under this type of duress – as if she'd been born with some kind of inner wisdom.

She rarely said anything, but 'Don't keep doing stupid things David', was conveyed in her stare. By and large, Jean and I got on quite well; of course at that time she hadn't made a take-over bid for my record player.

Mother's verbal onslaughts carried on for a few days, until the decomposing matter that represents a young lad's brain, went on holiday or switched itself off. If I remember correctly, her words of wisdom were absorbed more readily whilst checking in the mirror for spots, making sure my hair was something Ricky Nelson wouldn't be ashamed to walk out under and wondering who the lucky girl was going to be the next time that I had some money to spend.

The damage that we did to the village and some of its occupants was as nothing compared to the damage that *Oldham Council* was to inflict upon them in the not too distant future. The building of the two Sholver estates above the village was to put an abrupt and permanent end to the idyll that was the village of Moorside.

2

Elvis's songs appeared in my life fairly regularly around the year 1959. They'd been around for quite a while before that, but I hadn't really been listening; besides I'd seen an excerpt from one of his films on our new television and while I liked his songs, I wasn't overly impressed with him. Too many moving parts, a deformed lip and a fairly greasy hair do, he looked swarthy but that could have been attributed to the inadequacies of black and white film, before the advent of colour. I suppose there would be an element of carefully concealed jealousy concerning his attraction for many of the girls that I knew. He wasn't about to give up on me and kept sending his messages my way, until I went out and bought his record *Hound Dog /Blue Suede Shoes* that had been re-released on 45rpm disc. Forty-fives, as the small records were known, had fine grooves and their soft composition made them flexible, unlike the larger 33⅓rpm and 78rpm records, which were brittle and didn't take kindly to user abuse. Those records particularly disliked being dropped, demonstrating their displeasure by fragmenting themselves and any other records of the same type within the drop zone. I think that 78s and 33⅓ records were purchased from Law Swallows, the record shop on George Street in town. Woolworth's on High Street in the town centre sold cover-versions of most popular songs. The recording artists had names like Frank Dean, Billy Scott, Brenda Smith or Jean Blake, not names that singers would normally choose to enhance their careers, or society people get married to for that matter. The record company making the cover versions was named Embassy and the information label coloured a deep shade of red with silver lettering, they were cheaper than the original labels and you were better off with leprosy if anyone knew you'd bought one of them.

Like most teenagers I thought that I should have unrestricted access to the family money tree when I required something new. We didn't own one of those, which meant that I only bought a record with the appearance of Halley's comet. I can't remember which shop supplied the few 45s that I owned. I'm inclined to think it was a shop in either The Hilton or The Flack's Arcade that was the provider around that time. Popular records stayed on the jukeboxes much longer in those days, sometimes for months, even years, so the need to buy recordings was less pressing than it is today.

I've got records from that era that ended their useful life a pale shade of grey through constant use.

It wasn't unusual for the needle to expire, after very little use, on the new record players that appeared after those earlier wind-up models had found their way to the corporation tip. Buying a new needle could be something of a performance; sometimes it was easier to buy the whole cartridge complete with all three needles – those were required to play your various sizes of disc. If you bought anything new in the early days of transistor-powered entertainment and wanted replacement parts almost immediately, the shop assistants looked at you as if you'd asked them for an 88mm.self-propelled anti-tank gun.

'Can I have a 45 needle for a Dansette record player, please?'

'Whoa, now hold on a bit, you only bought the record player from here two months ago, there won't be many spare parts about just yet for new models, besides it takes about five weeks for new parts to get here, as with all new parts, it's the business of supply and demand.'

A short pause followed that speech, to see how the news was being received.

Record player owner asks tentative question, 'Well, can't you demand one then?'

Shop assistant replies, 'Er no, not really, they don't like a demand for parts of a new product, it upsets them'.

Disgruntled record player owner takes a few seconds to mull over the last sentence.

Thinking the chap is being clever, record player owner shouts with rage, splashing shop assistant who begins to look panicky.

'Upsets them, bloody well upsets them, I want a needle for a record player, not an engine for a bloody Rolls Royce'.

Shop assistant ducks under the deluge, searching through his trouser pockets for a handkerchief to mop his slightly damp face and then shrugs. 'Sorry, we only carry spare parts in stock for Philips and Bush models'.

Record player owner looks at shop assistant and gauges width of man's neck with a view to strangulation.

'You've only got spares for …' record player owner bellows, now on the verge of a mild seizure.

Shop assistant, sensing extreme distress in record player owner's demeanour and colouring, steps back one pace from the counter and looks in the direction of the manager's office – which is now empty.

An unspoken rude word hangs approximately two feet above the sales counter between the record player owner and shop assistant.

Record player owner sighs resignedly, tapping foot on floor and drumming fingers on the wooden counter, while searching his vocabulary for meaningful words – finding none that will fit the situation without being abusive. Turning his back to the assistant, he places an order for the spare part, thereafter grunting mild expletives under his breath, prefixing each whispered word with 'It'sabugger, intit?'

Nervous shop assistant thinks the faint words just spoken could be in Swahili.

Record player owner slams shop door closed on his way out, rattling the shop's tea-making equipment on a table near the exit, kicks at lamp-post base in front of the shop next door, hurting the toes of his right foot when the post doesn't seem inclined to budge. A rapidly-descending red mist clouds his vision as he limps to the bus stop outside The Artisan's Rest on Yorkshire Street, taunted by screaming hordes of kids heading for the Saturday afternoon matinée at the King's Cinema on Fairbottom Street. *(I couldn't play football that afternoon either)*.

Record player owner's girlfriend is unimpressed when he turns up that night at her front door, limping like a drunk with a shoe missing. His girlfriend is even less impressed when record player owner says irritably that she sounds like Long John Silver's parrot, squawking-on about the slow progress being made to the cinema. Record player owner doesn't spot the irony.

.

My first and only record player was a red-and-cream-coloured Dansette. It had two knobs on the outside of the front panel, the top one an On/Off switch incorporating the volume, the other a Bass/Treble switch with a range that ran from 'tinny' to a fairly high pitched whine. Any pretensions the set might have harboured about bass-sound could only have been in its imagination or in the extravagant claims of its manufacturers. Although adequate for my needs, it didn't come anywhere near the window-bulging noise produced by the vault-sized radiogram in Lawrie's house. Lawrie had three older sisters, Shirley, June and Pat, all of whom I really liked – they were great. When I called for Lawrie on our way out on Saturday nights I'd lean against their kitchen units trying to look cool – like you do when you're sixteen – while those three girls would be wafting past smelling of freshly-applied perfume, putting the finishing touches to make-up and singing along with whatever was coming out of their music machine. It was brilliant and we hadn't gone out yet. They were constantly testing the quality of the window putty in their front room by turning the volume knob up pretty high when nobody older was around the place. The machine had so much bass it jangled the empty cooking pans hanging in our pantry – we lived across the road from them. They had the full co-operation of Elvis Presley of whom they had every L.P. record on the market. Buddy Holly, Bill Haley, Conway Twitty and The Everly Brothers joined in the fun regularly. Apart from the in-house listeners, most of our neighbourhood was well versed in how good – or bad – life was, for a teenager in love. I wonder how many people of my generation are walking around slightly deaf from their inability to locate the volume control on the various noise boxes that they once owned. Take notice when you're out how many middle-aged people say 'Eh' after being asked a question.

If any of you have teenage children or grandchildren, there's no point in flying off the handle every time one of them decides that the people of Indonesia should listen-in, without benefit of a receiver, to what is playing on your television – especially the programme *Top Of The Pops*. There isn't anything wrong with them, apart from their individual peculiarities of course, it's just that it's your turn to have your nerves twanged a little.

3

There was an interim period, after we left our respective schools and before we ran out into the world, of coming to terms with a different way of life, work etc. We spent some time eavesdropping on the conversations of older youths, picking up tough phraseology, finding out where it was possible for the under-aged to get a drink of beer and where to find someone called Shesa Deadcert. If the eavesdropping hadn't taken place, we would eventually have succumbed to the town's primeval rhythms, anyway. While the tutorial was in progress we were all going to the pictures on Saturday nights, usually a horror film showing at the Gaumont Cinema, Union Street – opposite the Star Inn – or some clapped out film at the Empire Cinema on Waterloo Street. The Empire had a reputation for showing lower-level films and was only marginally better than the Victory Cinema near Rhodes Bank. I only went to 'The Vic' once; its principal feature was an upper level of seating (reputed to be made from orange boxes) spoken of as 'Sittin' up int' Gods'. The Empire employed a couple of bouncers, which was of no consequence when a full row of teenage lads (maybe twenty in all) decided to join in the chorus when the film was a musical. The two likely chaps and a few usherettes came flashing their torches in the direction of the unholy racket but if nobody looked at them they usually went away. Nobody's entertainment was spoiled, because the Empire was full of teenagers anyway; it was source of amusing distraction if the film was particularly bad. We once went to the Palladium cinema on Union Street to see a horror film, I think it was called *The Fall of the House of Usher*, or maybe *The House on Haunted Hill*, it was something Hitchcockian anyway. Towards the end of the film the principal male lunatic was scaring a woman into walking backwards unknowingly towards an acid bath. He was dangling a skeleton on a fishing rod line from out of her sight in order to achieve her demise. The cinema audience was in thrall and absolutely quiet. At that juncture a full sized imitation skeleton came rattling down on an, until then, invisible wire from the rear of the cinema to the front about eight feet above the audience. You can imagine the shrieking and uproar that went on while the blessed thing was clattering down the wire overhead from where it had been hidden behind a narrow curtain. I can tell you that there weren't many heads above seat height (including ours) and a few people were out in the aisles ready to leg it. Ho, ho, ho, I should think anyone with bowel problems was given immediate release and the event more than likely advanced a few coronary conditions. Ah dear! What passed as entertainment then would now be a reason to spend three months in the courts so that the film's makers could explain why half the population of the town was off work sick, with apprehensive stress or some other clap-trap excuse to be given money. The laxative qualities of the idea only worked on the opening night of the film because word swiftly got around and by the second night it only had a novelty interest. Not long after that episode, Lawrie met his lovely lady Kath, we all found the Savoy dancehall and The Odd House pub, but that's for later.

Eventually we were raring to go to town and were prepared, hopefully, to be corrupted, but not before we had been on holiday to Middleton Towers, a holiday camp near Morecambe. Sixteen-year old lads let off the leash for the very first time; it was like dieters being given the keys to a chocolate biscuit factory. On arrival our first mission was to learn how to sit at the rear tables in the Tudor Bar, nursing a large glass of beer and looking as if we had been doing it for years. It's a fact that at 16 years of age, you think the word 'maturity' applies to you, as well as to ripe cheese and old trees. You assume that your maturity is there for all to see, regardless of the fact that your face is full of cuts from your first efforts at shaving and you are eyeing up women in the bar old enough to be your mother. It's great until a couple of matrons decide to have some fun, testing your apparent interest by approaching your table. Then it's a case for drinking up and legging it with your newfound maturity tucked away in your back pocket.

Partway through the holiday some girls made themselves available and because experience hadn't yet taught anyone the rudiments of kissing, the lads tried to swallow them whole. You'll know how it goes, find the lips and stick yourself firmly to them, taking occasional breaks for oxygen, meals and drinking.

Amongst the camp's amusements was one of those old punch ball machines. It was the type that requires a penny in the slot, which then allows you to pull the punch ball down. The ball is suspended from a foot-long piece of thin chain. A bell rings on the machine if you are strong enough to punch the ball into the middle of next week. Eight stone being our average weight, bursting paper bags was just about our limit in the punching game. Optimism is a shining light in the endeavours of young people and Terry worked out a way of making the machine's bell ring. His idea was to pull down the punch ball, march across the narrow passageway to the other side, lift the punching hand to shoulder height and launch yourself at the machine on the run, punching the ball as you arrived – the idea worked wonderfully well, ringing the bell. That day the bell was asked to ring far more than was good for it and it kept on ringing until we were just about knackered. It worked at 11pm too, much to the irritation of those living nearby hoping for an early night in bed. The following night the machine was disconnected and stayed so until the next morning. Towards the end of our first week the bell was quite hoarse and reduced to making faint buzzing noises because of overuse.

You'll know about adults spoiling your fun I suppose. One day a largish young man with a baby perched on his arm had been watching our performance with interest. He walked slowly up to the machine in true gunfighter style, with baby still sitting on his arm. Pulling the ball down with one hand he gave it a lusty thwack with the same fist, without disturbing the baby or his hair, the bell rang its noisy little head off. Somewhere in the finer detail, maybe our technique needed a bit of working on.

I don't know how others have been affected by mealtimes in a holiday camp, but my introduction to them was a bit of a face stiffener. Great growling noises and cutlery banging filled the huge hall. Segregation from other diners was the order of the day, provided by a blanket of cigarette smoke, swirling lazily amongst the tables. The dinner or tea menu, depending upon which part of the country you hail from, was comprised largely of salad. The meal arrived on your plate in a variety of styles; the components only differing in the quantity of each item present and the shade of green. Favoured entertainment during mealtimes was propping your head up on your arm to idly watch lettuce leaves, being carried by live protein, make progress round your plate. Breakfast had to be taken wearing sunglasses in order to minimise the glare coming from your plate, there was enough grease running around it to give a flock of vultures indigestion. If you had been drinking the previous evening, a considerable amount of will power had to be exercised before making the first tentative move towards your cutlery. Sausages, eggs and under-cooked strands of bacon stared up from your plate in defiance, daring you to take the initial step. Fried bread had an air of disinterest about it, knowing it would get its own back on you, via indigestion, in approximately one hour's time. Far-sighted fried bread with a game plan, aimed to get you in forty years' time and I've no doubt accomplished the feat, with willing assistance along the way from its savoury accomplices in the chip shop. Just imagine, millions of calories scrambling to board food-delivery trucks, squeaking with delight when they found cooking lard or beef dripping in the cargo. Ho, ho, ho! Today's greasy-food critics would down a few pints of yoghurt and lentil soup, dig out their vitamin-enriched track suits and run a dozen laps round the park at the mere thought of such fare being available for consumption.

Entertainment in the evenings consisted in the main, of ex-club singers and groups doing their stuff in the ballroom. Sweating men – jackets off and down to their braces – danced with their partners until they were too slippery to hold, in the heat from the overhead lighting. Lights were always switched on in entertainment rooms, even if there was still a couple of daylight hours left. Were you in the vicinity of one of the social clubs you could be in for a treat, when half a dozen beer-filled men on stage showed their audience what the Lord had given them in order to take part in a knobbly-knees contest. Ah, but that was all too rich for us, we took ourselves off to the Tudor Bar thinking that a good dousing in beer and the possibility of being ill from it, was the better way to spend time. There was usually a comedian working in the bar who told jokes rude enough to make an infantryman blush – well maybe not that rude, say a builder's labourer or a Premier League footballer.

Ingemar Johansson was fighting Floyd Patterson on the radio one night during our holiday; well the fight was held at three o'clock in the morning. (They weren't actually fighting, on the radio, if you know what I mean). We stayed up to listen to the fight and the girls were there too. With regard to the chalets, non-fraternisation with girls who weren't related to you was the byword; anyone caught *in flagrante* would be thrown off the camp on his, her, or their ear, so said a dozen notices pinned around the chalets. The chalets were two and four berth and not meant to accommodate eight or so loud teenagers. That being so, the inevitable happened sooner rather than later. While we were waiting for the fight to commence, chalet patrol visited us after someone had complained about the noise. We quickly selected the one amongst us who could tell white lies without blinking an eye and Terry went to answer the door. A cock-and-bull story, the likes of which I may never hear again was given – the girls were crammed in a dark corner hardly daring to breathe while the palaver was going on.

Terry said someone was ill and we had sent for the camp's medical practitioner to attend the unfortunate one (someone inside groaned periodically). It was a long convoluted explanation that even a politician would have had difficulty delivering, however it did the trick. Keeping ourselves quiet after the visit was nothing short of medal-worthy – quite inspirational for youngsters like us. Maybe there was a bit of fear behind that – ejection from the camp being the main concern.

In those days, people weren't of the nature to force an entrance to establish if you were speaking the truth, even those with a perfect right to do so. Maybe it's the likes of our generation that have brought about the current trend to disbelieve anything that anyone says. There was a willingness to trust in most people until proven otherwise. The nanny state is upon us these days and delves into our psyche on the weakest pretext. We need to know everything yesterday; more prevention is better than just prevention – which we all know, is better than cure. Save the criminal, sod the offended, seems to be the way of things.

I have this 'hobby-horse' and it ticks me off no end, it is 'Early Learning' for children. What the hell for? What's the rush? Given that we have approximately 80 years to learn in, why do we need to know everything as soon as we step from the womb? Pretty soon babies will join us clutching half a dozen G.C.S.E.s and be able to tell you how many times Cara Farmer-Trumpington has fallen into the social mire.

In today's society, if you get a spell in your finger they send for an ambulance, drag a timber specialist from his favourite tree, an orthopaedic consultant off the top of his money-pile and you have to write your life's history on twenty sheets of foolscap paper – with such enquiries as, 'where did you take your last holiday?', 'do you pay income tax at the full rate?', 'are you in any way related to Abou Ben Adhem?' and say if your parents were addicted to the Smurfs or Chicken Chow Mein in the nineteen seventies.

I know, I know, it's the age thing and I can whinge with the best of them.

I didn't listen to the title fight because I fell asleep during the preliminaries.

I've watched a few generations of teenagers set foot on the trail in their search for Utopia since those days. By and large they succumb to the same primeval urges that we did. Although it affects each new generation in different ways, the Pied Piper of Immaturity lures them all eventually.

We easily located the genesis-bus, a mythical vehicle built to carry the annual pilgrimage of the nation's spotty youth and being thus seduced; we broke our uncaring necks to get on it. In an advanced state of excitement and with no inhibitions whatsoever we told the figurative bus driver, 'Into town, my man, and give it some stick'. Real buses from all parts of the Borough would converge on the town-centre at round about the same time each weekend. These would be half-filled with movie or singing star replicas, trying to appear disinterested in everything, unsure what it was that they were suppressing or why. Well, I can tell them, they're squashing down a condition that normally manifests itself in high spirits or exuberance but it's un-cool to show it, so I'm told. It's one of those fleeting things in life and something that I haven't enjoyed for a while – at least I don't think I have. (It's an oddity the way that youth cannot abide older or much younger people, yet gather together a few teenagers in a single room and they get along as happily as vicars at a christening).

We caught the fabled bus regularly until we were sure of the way to the Stygian flames that the majority of youth dances round. To paraphrase Sir Edmund Hillary from the peak of Mount Everest – it was all down hill from there on in.

4

First let me give you a bit of our early history. Lawrie and I had been educated at Henshaw's Secondary Modern, a Church of England school (the Blue Coat School as it was previously, and is now known), Terry and Bob attended St. Anselm's Roman Catholic School, which along with Derker Secondary Modern School, Hulme Grammar School, Greenhill Grammar School, Counthill Grammar School, Hathershaw Technical College and ours, were the main senior-pupil schools in the town at the time. Religion was never on the agenda in our friendship, other than the religious application of the pleasure gene. Some of our classmates lived in the town centre; they knew the ropes with regard to the attractions of the town, passing on much interesting information in our final year, which we duly stored for imminent use.

Aged fifteen, complete with the first line of a love-pedigree, which I had acquired aged fourteen after a hasty and unenlightening very, very, short incursion into the method of procreation (the incident embarrassed us both) I was ready for what was on offer. So venturing into the work place I had already had a practice start with the ladies and I felt as if I was armed and dangerous.

Oldham in the late nineteen fifties had many clothing, clothing-accessory and footwear shops that sold a better-than-average quality of goods: Jolly's, Hardcastle's, Salter's, Flack's, Weston's, Halon Shirts, Peover's, Dunne & Co, Greenwood's, Ann Collier, Beatrice Isles, to name a few; there will be others that I've forgotten about. Everyone was in work at that time and there was plenty of money around to support a good class of merchandise. There was also a large choice of furniture and audio businesses, in Buckley and Procter, Lloyd's, Woodhouse's, Mann's, and Wildebore's. I'm pretty sure that Ardern's curtain and soft furnishings shop opened at the top of Curzon Street, replacing Cooper's hat/cap shop. Cooper's had a novel method for attracting customers to their boys' wear section. Their Curzon Street display window was filled with three rows of boys' school caps in their various colours, types and sizes, each displaying a shiny penny on top of the cap. The child got the penny if a cap was purchased from

25

the shop; a penny was a lot of money for a youngster. If you had nothing better to do with your time, you could stand nearby and witness mothers being dragged around the pavement outside the shop by whingeing, penny-wanting boys, particularly during the summer holidays as a new school term was approaching

The workplace that was unfortunate enough to provide my first stint in harness was Phil Cohen at the top of Curzon Street where it meets Albion Street. The shop was situated on the outside corner of Victoria Market next to the Fruit and Vegetable stalls. (Victoria Market was variously known as the Outside Market, the Covered Market or the Market Hall.) The business was in direct competition with Alexander's, Jackson's, Montague Burton's and John Collier's, all tailors, situated on High Street and Market Place. Phil Cohen was generally reckoned to sell clothing of a superior quality to the other establishments. On the male side of things in the shop there was the manager who amongst his many other attributes had been a Special Constable in the ranks of Oldham Police (he sounded as though he had enjoyed himself in his part-time occupation, some of the details of which could be subject to a defamation claim from any of his progeny or any of their progeny come to that, so I won't be retelling them here). Amongst his non-litigious reminiscences, he told us of the time he was on night duty with a full-time constable and witnessed a mass migration of rats crossing High Street from Flack's Arcade; he said the pack must have stretched from top to bottom of the arcade. The tale might have been stretched a little because he said that the Woodman public house on Lord Street had a welcoming back door which was unlocked until one o'clock or so in the morning, and policemen with nothing much to do…. The rats he spoke of, apparently went down the side street separating Yates's Wine Lodge outdoor licence and Alexander's the tailors and scampered through the railings of St. Peter's Church graveyard. He didn't say which part of the year the incident took place, maybe they fancied a week's R&R in Ashton or were dining out at Hollinwood Market hoping for a better class of cuisine. He never mentioned a piper or the town of Hamelin either.

At that time and until comparatively recently, unwanted vegetables, discarded hot food, and general waste from the market was stored in a large brick building next to the Outside Market Public Toilets, which in turn was situated next to Lever's Fish Market on Albion Street. In that corner of the outside market it was difficult to decide which smelled worse, the market rubbish tip, Lever's Fish Market or the take-away hot black puddings stall, run by a very large lady who was a living advertisement for the goodness in her product. The combination of aromas was thoroughly disgusting. If the local authority was unable to remove the rubbish each market day for any reason, the stuff stayed there until the next morning. The town centre wasn't as squeaky clean as it is today with compaction skips and mechanised sweepers making the cleaning tasks much easier. Cardboard and other forms of detritus would be left outside the rear of shop premises, sometimes over the weekend. This was apparent in the mounds of wrapping rubbish left around The Green, a piece of open ground on Albion Street that was home to a few children's roundabouts and the odd vagrant in transit.

The other male person in the shop was a salesman in his late twenties who moved on to work somewhere else not long after my arrival. Terry, a young man fresh from doing his National Service in the army, who had worked in the shop before starting his stint in the army, replaced him. He had some really interesting stories about his army times in Germany. Even now I can recall a chap he nicknamed 'Lindana' Ben (the spelling may be incorrect), Lindana being a brand of German beer. Apparently Ben was engaged in a quest to drink dry all of West Germany, with an option to do the same to the lower reaches of the Austrian Tirol. If he had enough time left before he expired, he was going to set about the northern part of Italy, with one eye firmly fixed on neighbouring France – drinking his way home in fact. We had some good laughs Terry and I, he was a likeable bloke, if it's possible to like someone else when you're sixteen. He had a fondness for traditional jazz – Kenny Ball, Acker Bilk, Chris Barber, Johnnie Dankworth and others I'm not familiar with – throwing his head back and simulating a clarinet or trumpet player each time a jazz record was played on the shop's small transistor radio. The transistor radio was hidden on a table behind some clothes racks in the shop. Should anyone wishing to purchase clothing have stumbled into the shop during these performances; they could have been forgiven for walking back outside to read the shop's nameplate above the front window. At times the noises floating out of the front door of the shop sounded like a foot-stompers' festival in the backwoods of Kentucky. He laughed along with me at his enthusiastic portrayals, but he was a real devotee of jazz and declared its virtues at any given opportunity. Still, nobody's perfect are they?

I recall times when people came into the shop, usually ladies with a gaggle of small children in tow, asking if the shop took clothing cheques. Those were commercial cheques for a specific amount of money to be spent wherever businesses would accept them. Finance companies issued the cheques to people who were unable to pay cash for their families' needs in apparel. Of the many companies that were in the business, the only ones that I can recall are the Bee Clothing Company and the Refuge Clothing Company. Our manager, a Cohen family member, was usually the first line of communication with the bearer of the cheque because he was warming his backside leaning against a yard-high, copper-coloured, storage heater, situated opposite the shop door on the first floor. From that vantage point he could see the length of Albion Street in the direction of Lord Street in the reflection in the shop's angled, front display window. The manager would say, in a lowered voice that he did take cheques, steering the lady into a quiet corner to find out if the cheque was issued by one of the companies that Phil Cohen dealt with. If so, the cheque vanished temporarily under the counter until business had been completed. Presumably shops of distinction didn't advertise the fact that they took your money in any other way than in cash. (Totally at odds with today's dealings, where a person can buy stuff with a piece of exotic looking plastic that isn't necessarily their own to begin with). Terry and I found it quite amusing to say in a brusque manner – particularly if there were other customers in the shop – ' 'course we do luv, what company is it?' Humph, that didn't go down well with the manager, I can tell you, but it supplied us with an hour or so of amusement. The manager was a past master of the pen-chucking strop and spent the last hour of that day scouring the employment ads. in the *Oldham Evening Chronicle* – I always thought he was trying to find us jobs. The man was a good bloke really. If we became bored at any time, one of us would start him off on the war and then we could switch off and doze a little.

On the female side of staff in the shop there was a 'Saturday girl/woman' in her early twenties, she dressed beautifully and bore a remarkable resemblance to Ava Gardner. She was a bit shiny and I'd have paid for a trip to the cinema, even at her age. Unfortunately she was only interested in the first salesman who was married and who, when asked to do his National Service had chosen the R.A.F., which I suppose elevated him above anyone else likely to be in contention for her admiration.

A trainee seamstress called into the shop most mornings on her way to work at the Rock Street branch of Cohen's, which was the dress-making, made-to-measure clothing side of the business. The tailors worked on the upper floor of the shop. I recall that the firm gave excellent personal service to customers, with the tailor who was making the garment standing in attendance whenever a fitting was required. (Today if you dare to comment about the fit of a pair of trousers, a staff member is quite likely to tell you that it isn't their fault if you're the wrong shape for the trousers). It turned out that the youngster had an interest in me – or so a male member of staff informed me – which, while exciting, was also a means of my getting a bit warm under the collar. I was fifteen she was seventeen, possibly eighteen, and good-looking; she scared me to death she was so sophisticated. There is a "stupid" gene virulent amongst teenage lads. I harboured this gene; therefore her interest was not about to bear fruit with any assistance from me. She was exceptionally pretty, what can I say. Still, at fifteen I had many optimistic irons in the fire with regard to girls and my acquiring one occasionally.

On Fridays and Saturdays a very important little man would pop into the shop just after lunchtime. A series of nods and questioning raised eyebrows between him and the manager would follow his silent entry to the premises. If the shop were empty of customers, a piece of paper and some money would be passed from the manager to Harry, the little man. Harry would pull out a pocket book and scribble into it what I presume was a copy of the note's contents and then he'd ghost out of the shop without so much as a by your leave. If the shop had customers he wouldn't enter but would re-appear a short time later when the coast was clear. He never came back once he'd done the business. Harry, a short slim man of fifty-odd who wore glasses and was dressed to blend, was a "bookies' runner". When I first observed those weekend customs, I, being fifteen, wondered if what took place was a rite or some sort of ceremonial custom to do with the Buff's (Royal Antediluvian Order of the Buffaloes), knowing that the manager was a member of that institution whose premises were situated at the top of Henshaw Street. When I queried the man's furtive doings, I was informed that the practice of "running for bookies" was against the law. That led me to speculate whether the "runner" part of the man's title meant he was running with bets into the bookies on Church Terrace all day long, or if he was expected to run away from the police if they decided to nab him.

At that time there were two older women of interest in my life and they both caught the 8.30a.m. bus from Moorside to Oldham. In a manner of speaking I had them both to myself. The bus was empty upstairs, all the school children getting off in the village, while anyone else using buses had been at work for half a day by the time I set out at 8.30a.m.

There was one exception to that surmise. A white-haired old man walking from the direction of Roebuck Lows caught the bus one day each week, although he shouldn't really count because he got off before the two ladies boarded it. He was approximately five feet four inches tall, slightly bandy-legged and rather than buckle up the belt to his raincoat, he tied it round his middle in a knot. He was only memorable because he smoked "Black Twist" pipe tobacco in a battered pipe that had "Methuselah" stamped on the bowl. Black Twist was a short, half-inch round or square, length of tobacco that had to be cut into small slices and rubbed in the palms of one's hands before being stuffed into the pipe's bowl. It didn't half pong once the smoker had got up a full head of steam. (My Dad smoked it once in the house in his pipe-smoking days – mother had an apoplectic fit and ran around the house theatrically throwing open all the windows). The man walked to the front of the bus and fired up his pipe, puffing away until he'd completely vanished. He reappeared when it was time to get off in the next village, emerging from his smoke screen with a dazed expression and a look of contentment on his face. Ho, ho, ho! He'd have been summarily deported or had a government health warning stamped on his forehead in these days of antipathy towards any kind of emission, human or otherwise.

Finding myself with nothing to do recently and speaking of a healthy life style, I asked myself, 'Will I live to be 85 years old if I've taken all the health advice I've been given or read about in my life?' According to my reckoning, which is based mainly on fried potatoes consumed and gallons of alcohol tippled, I should do it easily with a month or two to spare.

Using the Rotunda calculation, which is, divide 2% of body weight into 50kg of potatoes, er, let me see, that's half a field full, and times that by chip shops visited between 1958 and 1993, less potato peel, insect holes and the Brussels calorific intake thingy, the sum of which equates roughly to three tonnes of chips consumed so far – nothing to speak of there then.

For beer I've used the Australian plonk slurpers' calculation, namely, 10 pints of Foster's leg deadener or 6 litres of Shiraz vin rogue, times by the amount of public toilets to be found in the city of Brisbane, add the combined I.Q. of the national Australian Rugby League team, deducting a little of that when no one's looking. Multiply that by home runs scored in Australia's last cricket Test Match against England down under, and the amount permissible to achieve my goal should be approximately the Newby Bridge end of Lake Windermere. Adhering to those rules for a healthy lifestyle will all have been a waste of course, if I ever forget the other one about walking along railway lines in the dark.

The first woman caught the bus at Highfield Terrace in Moorside and came up the stairs; she must have been all of twenty-five years old, her hair was a lovely shade of honey blonde, she always wore fitted two-piece suits and high heeled shoes – sometimes she changed the effect by adding an umbrella if it was raining. The lady was tall with a good figure and she regularly sat near the front of the bus. She always smiled at me as she arrived at the top of the stairs and again as she walked back to alight at Hill Stores. I was dead chuffed; nearly every working morning this happened to me. My Sugar Frosties couldn't come out of their box fast enough and I must have eaten every shade of toast that a grill can provide for breakfast in my hurry to get visually presentable. Don't we, as kids, have a fairly narrow perspective though? It occurred to me in later years that if you're a smiling type of person, then you smile at whatever you've got available. Umm, that would have been me. I had a six-month love affair with the lovely lady; sadly she never knew about it. Something similar in practice to my father-in-law, who falls out with people but neglects to inform them of the fact.

The next girl was about nineteen. "Sinuous", "flowing", "willowy", "sultry" all of those things applied to her. She was so visible she must have been plugged into the electricity mains each morning. This girl boarded the bus at Alva Road, the next bus stop down from the first woman's. Both bus stages are on Ripponden Road. The girl had straight dark hair and one of those modern, magazine-cover faces. You'll know the type, looks as if she's accidentally swallowed her engagement ring, or she's sitting on something excruciatingly sharp. She usually wore a black, flared, shorty-length, Astrakhan topcoat with a big hide-your-ears fur collar, the lapels held together with one hand just below her chin. She didn't come upstairs on the bus; it's likely that she couldn't climb the blessed things and always got off at Magneto Services on Union Street, the bus stop just before Brunswick Street. From the back seat of the bus, ladies with visual merit were observed keenly as the bus pulled away from the stop. On nice days with the early sun behind her, she looked superb swaying along in her extra-high-heeled shoes. All the best crooners of the day burst into song as she walked her measured unhurried pace. She must have known she looked good by the amount of times my happy little well-scrubbed face appeared in the rear window of the bus. I often received a secretive smile. It's surprising what little your ego can live on when you're young. The Lord knows what would have happened if she had ever fallen off those heels – more to the point who would have had to cough up for the replacement of the broken flags. Either of those two ladies would have swallowed me up as if I had been a canapé after a week-long diet, had I ever been given the chance to fulfil my ambitions.

The rear seats on the upstairs of a bus were always preferred, if available, to the other seats. You could survey the rest of the deck without restriction. When tired of waiting for an ogle-worthy girl to appear, you could open the emergency-exit door behind the seat and shout slanderous remarks or flirt your bus ticket at lads you knew. Trying to explain the latter action to an advancing ticket inspector when the ticket had long since flown, wasn't an experience to look forward to. There have been times when I've got off the bus rather than face embarrassment when caught ticketless. I knew that swearing on a stack of bibles or referring him to my impeccable lineage wouldn't convince the man that I had paid my fair. Alan, an older lad from our village and a bus conductor, gave me a free ticket one day when I told him that I'd genuinely lost my ticket and the ticket inspector was about to introduce me to his working footwear while assisting me from the bus. In doing so, my saviour refuted the allegation that most bus conductors were dictatorial morons.

I was to be a tailor eventually – or so my mother had said. I m not sure that the shop owners agreed with her, at least they never mentioned it to me. Her choice of my occupation didn't sit happily on my shoulders I can tell you. My status as trainee whatever-I-was-to-be didn t last long – twelve months maybe. In that time I found that I wasn't cut out to be subservient to the whims of the callous-free, or to pasty-faced propriety and to make the disaffection more immediate I was decidedly unhappy about taking the inside-leg measurements of men buying trousers. Worst of all I had to work Saturdays; alright I got Tuesday afternoon off work, a fat lot of good that was when all my mates were working. Regardless of those job-shortcomings I met a few lads about town, one of whom was Mike a youngster of my age who worked at Peover's a men's outfitters, the next shop but one along Albion Street. He stayed with the firm many a long year. There was also a cool, unsmiling girl who worked for Hyde's, Stationers and Newsagents in the Market Hall opposite the rear of Peover's shop – Jackie appears later in the book.

The rest of my mates became bricklayers, engineers and followed other manual occupations; those were men's jobs according to my dad. All was not wasted in my time at the shop as it turned out. On the plus side I learned the value of wearing good quality clothing and the nature of the job meant I had to be of clean appearance; they were necessary lessons that have served me well. Much more importantly though, I was in a perpetual state of sartorial readiness should any good-looking girl be interested in me as a prospective date for the evening. Later on, when I had found my way around the system a bit, some girls were interested. So started my tenure as a self-appointed, know-everything, cosmopolitan, hotshot. If we are completely honest, most of us thought the person looking back at us from the bathroom mirror couldn't be improved upon, didn't we? Ha, ha, ha, we were conceited sods and no mistake, me particularly and for no good reason that I can think of. It baffles me still; self-delusion was a place that I must have visited regularly.

5

Right, here's roughly how our transition from foolish to coolish began. We were an eager group of four, wet behind the ears, knowing a lot about nothing and ready to be entertained by that ancient Lancashire recreation known as 'avinagoodtime'. The finger of fear and fulfilment was beckoning and we weren't exactly reticent about following it, now that it had made itself known. We began by observing the weekend nocturnal activities of our peers who were diving regularly into the bowels of the town, only resurfacing when they had a new girlfriend or had achieved a fair degree of intoxication, the latter changing them into people less belligerent than they were when sober.

Having learned over a period of weeks the basics for survival, we ran at the town stamping all over its welcome mat and no doubt, some of its institutions. We were swallowed immediately and to the casual observer, vanished without trace, merging with that year's spotty intake. During this early period of my adjustment from adolescent to adult, I was unencumbered by the need to go out with just any girl. On our third visit to the Savoy dancehall, a pretty girl named Margaret who lived in the village of Waterhead showed her excellent selective qualities by inviting me out on a date. The hot message was delivered by her friend – it was normal for the times. I'd noticed her and her friends standing near the glass partition at the top of the front staircase, sorting out the possible from the probable male candidates on show. Thinking that they were way out of my league, I walked on by. In choosing me for instant stardom (more likely it was beginner's luck) she contributed greatly to my excitable portfolio. The girl was more experienced in matters to do with courting than I was, telling me that she had recently dated a singer in a rock 'n' roll band – I was impressed. I had been quite impressed from the start of the encounter because two of my mates, who considered themselves to be over-subscribed in the art of "chatting-up", had got nowhere with her. She was a nice girl, very happy and bubbly, everybody liked her. I was so chuffed that I went out and bought an Elvis record to commemorate the occasion: *Are You Lonesome Tonight*. (I thought I was being hugely extravagant, I only got one pound a week pocket money – while Elvis probably got the price of a tiny rivet for his next new Cadillac). I was impressed with myself; this was my first real girlfriend, somebody to have on my arm and I was an eager learner in the subtle art of lip tasting.

Impressed? 'Course I was impressed, I was levitating! Hmm, and then I made a classic misjudgement. We arrived in Margaret's street one night, after a couple of weeks' going-out and having a rush of blood so to speak, I wondered if we might advance the relationship a little. That was beautifully parried by Margaret's use of the classic counter, 'My dad waits up for me, I have to be in by eleven o'clock.'

I went home in a huff as only a sixteen year old can, walking home past Strinesdale reservoirs in the pitch darkness rather than walk through Watersheddings and Moorside, my expensive Italian suede shoes taking their first and only steps into mud and cow muck. I spent the whole of the journey bumping into tree branches and falling over the cast-iron ends of the benches situated alongside the pathways. After finally sprawling headlong over a crumbling field wall by a wooden footbridge over the valley's small stream, I arrived home. I was pretty-well tee'd off by that time, my rip-your-arm-off temper poised on the brink of sanity, waiting for someone to be smirkingly critical of my appearance and I recall being really disappointed when nobody was. I'd lost my comb – the only thing of value for my daily maintenance – the knees to my trousers were the same shade of green as the elbows to my off-white, cotton-poplin, "Shortie" rain coat and I'd exhausted my store of swear words. I should have known at the outset of the night that it was going to be a bad one when Ginger haughtily refused to relinquish my dad's fireside chair so that I could brush-up my suede shoes, even though my mother's chair was available to me. Pointing towards the kitchen and saying 'Gerinyerbasket' or brandishing a rolled newspaper usually did the trick. Ah well, he was an awkward little sod at times. His refusal didn't involve any loss of face on my part because everyone else in the house was watching after-tea telly in the front room. Starting off a pedigree in seduction can be very, very stressful.

Margaret's best friend handed me a note on the next dance-night at the Savoy. There being no psychobabble expert around to counsel me on emotional scarring or whatever the shrinks call it these days, I didn't read the note, theatrically tearing it up before casually showering the residue onto the cobbles at the side of the dancehall. I thought about retrieving the pieces after her friend had gone back inside the Savoy to report on my misjudgement, but I didn't. Always read your mail before binning it. That note could have been my passport to Utopia. I didn't think about that at the time though, my brains were obviously in the wrong place. You'll know by now, that any depth to my character can be measured in millimetres. In peevish mode and prone to bouts of image cherishing, I'd decided the blame for my predicament lay with Margaret's dad. For all I know the man could have been tucked up in bed fast asleep, blissfully unaware of the muddy little drama that I had starred in, while crossing Winterbottom's lower meadows. Like all teenagers, I couldn't possibly be the cause of my own discomfort and the laundry bills had to be paid by someone – as it turned out, that someone was yours truly. I'd given my mother a short, sanitised version of the story but she still declined to pay for the cleaning, refusing my offer of eternal gratitude, on the grounds of disloyalty to fellow women. (Rascally women at both ends of the age spectrum. Huh, talk about being ganged-up on.) With regard to the petulant paper tearing, when young everyone carries his or her irritations around in a fairly large sack, sometimes the neck isn't tied up properly and you spill a few. That's just how it is.

From the time of our leaving school, the town-centre was the pivot around which life's diversions revolved. Even the air in town was slightly intoxicating and a subdued tingle of excitement went hand in hand with a feeling of expectation. Loud music accompanied us everywhere we turned, everything we did seemed to be accompanied by rock 'n' roll music. It wove its way through the crowded streets, providing the background to our leisure time, seeping out of the constantly opening pub doors from their big, bass-biased Rock-ola, Wurlitzer, Seeburg or BAL-AMi jukeboxes. At weekends the shops were full of Saturday people spending. I could almost smell the cotton-oil and engineering money vanishing into the town's cash registers. You could hardly make progress sometimes without treading on someone's toes or falling over someone's small child or their dog, the place was so crowded.

Speaking of dogs (you may not wish to know this small fact but I'll tell you anyway), a tall, well-dressed, elderly gentleman and a lady of some refinement, who was attached by a lead to a small dog, were enjoying discourse one sunny afternoon outside Walker's Fish Shop on Albion Street. After a period of sniffing around the pavement the dog decided to christen the rear of the man's trouser leg. Presumably because no retribution seemed to be forthcoming, it ran round the other side of the man and went for a matching pair. The old man didn't bat an eyelid or show any sign of distress at the treatment to his apparel. While we watched, the dog tried someone else's leg (maybe before its tank ran dry). The leg belonged to a man selling shoelaces from a tray hung around his neck. Unfortunately for the dog, the man was closely observing his immediate surroundings and wearing boots. With the well-timed swing of one of them, he lifted the hapless hound approximately two feet from the ground. The dog's owner let out an unsophisticated screech as she felt the leash tighten, bringing the dog's heavenward flight to a sudden stop. The old man seemed to get a little alarmed and stepped back a pace or two. Surging into action the lady set about the shoelace-seller forgetting that the dog was suffering from an aborted take-off. Meanwhile, the dog was busy trying to plot a course for Rochdale before it was subjected to further in-flight turbulence. After two minutes of handbag whacking, leg puncing and dog yelping the combatants drew apart, giving the shoelace vendor time to scuttle off down Curzon Street and safety. Conversation with the old chap cut short, the good lady marched off down Market Avenue dragging the dog along behind. She was airborne with fury and I'd venture that she and her dog were six inches off the ground for the first three yards. The scene still gives me pleasure today and is capable of inducing horrendous hiccoughs. I know, I know, it was unfortunate for the dog, although it was trying to acquire territory that it didn't hold title too.

The scene during hostilities was similar to the one where I imagine a fox enters the hen-house intent upon securing lunch and pandemonium ensues. Ah well, it's good for an attack of the giddys on a 'Remember when...' visit – call it amusement therapy.

For most people, Saturday was the one day when pleasure was given free rein from the distractions of work and people anticipated its arrival. The day was a kaleidoscope of events. Everyone poured into town getting their once-weekly enjoyment fix. Not like today's humdrum shopping where we have Monday to Sunday inclusive and every day is the same-old, same-old...

6

Owing to continual disenchantment with my working hours, I was obliged to terminate my employment with Phil Cohen. The pay wasn't spectacular either. I think my first wage was £2. 7s. 6p. (£2.37½p). I had to work 44 hours per week for that – well, I attended the premises. The following week I found myself sitting on a leather chair in a well-appointed office waiting to be interviewed for the position of junior assistant in the inspection office of Whitworth Mallinson, of Royton, sheet metal manufacturers. Royton was independent of Oldham Council at that time and a bit like another country to bumpkins like me. Amongst its many metal fabricating activities, the company produced ducting for aircraft engines on contract for Lucas Gas Turbines (I'm not sure about the Gas Turbines part of their title). Prior to the interview with Mr. Whitworth, who was a nice man or seemed to me to be, I had hauled out and polished my stock answer to one of the questions standard for the day at interview, one that I knew he would ask me.

The question that always popped up towards the end of interviews was, 'Why do you think I should give you the job above the other applicants?'

'Because I'm adaptable and although I wasn't the brightest kid in our class, I wasn't the dumbest either.' For some reason it slayed them, I didn't know why then and I still don't.

It was verging on being a lie too; depending upon which part of dumbest you are O.K with. I like to think that the thought-provoking, half-aggrandisement got me the job. The work was interesting for a while and the firm was a good employer. Unfortunately the job required those few brain cells that I keep on duty, to acquit themselves in a diligent and orderly manner. True to form for me, those cells were always in direct competition with the cells that represent idleness, carelessness and sloth. The latter were the principal architects of my undoing. One of the company's welders played football or had played, for a local team, Haggate Lads. He was a much more interesting prospect than finding flaws in the welding of aircraft ducting or trying to work out the settings of a Vernier or height gauge, in order to get an object to correspond with a set of draughtsman's drawings. Some nine months or so later, after an extended period of mutual disenchantment, the shop floor manager and I had a little chat, during which I gathered that although my contribution to the firm was much appreciated, I would be better employed elsewhere. I should try to get a job more in line with my talents and would I make some haste to find one with that point of view in mind. Incidentally, the position that I held was previously owned by one Malcolm George later to become Chief Constable of Oldham, who also left the firm early in his career, so I was in good company – he left voluntarily of course. So there I was, gradually working my way down the employment ladder from jobs with good prospects to jobs that required the mental resources of half a field full of goats. Work and therefore financial salvation came from Tony, the lad who lived next door to us, but more of that later.

My mates had enjoyed Saturday afternoons in town for the past twelve months, indeed since my commencement at Phil Cohen and the requirement to work on Saturdays. Now at sixteen and a half years old with a new five-day-week job in my pocket, I joined them. The afternoons sometimes started with us dropping off the bus (literally) at the top of George Street and walking across Market Place, passing a tiny tobacconist-cum-newsagents (who would sell you five Domino cigarettes in an open-ended pack with two matches, apparently they tasted like dried camel manure – or so I'm told) near to Burton's tailors, before turning up Curzon Street, dodging the buskers, trumpet players, bootlace sellers, tin-can rattlers, dodgy traders et al. There were various forms of vocal street entertainment during the day, one I remember particularly issuing from a tall chap who wore a large overcoat and walked up and down Curzon Street bellowing his lungs out at the top of his voice – unaccompanied by music. To do that takes some nerve, or a lack of it; he was probably a fine baritone to those less ignorant than us. At our age it was an opportunity to snigger and nudge each other as we passed by him in the street. He'd obviously never heard of Ricky Nelson, Del Shannon, or Eddie Cochran, why else would he be making such an unholy racket? I tell you, as a youngster, your patience was on the same level as that afforded to a bucket full of beach pebbles.

These days, I'm a convert to some types of classical singing, with a liking for the voice of Andrea Bocelli. It's a contentious statement I know, but you've never heard anyone sing anything until you've heard Bocelli sing the Schubert version of Ave Maria. With regard to classical music I'm not into anything heavy: Tarrega's *Memories of Alhambra*, Samuel Barber's *Adagio for Strings*, Canteloube's *Songs of the Auvergne* and the 'crossover' music of guitar player Gustavo Montesano make me happy. Mind you I still get interested when I hear Jerry Lee Lewis hammering his piano into trauma, gleefully squeezing out *Whole Lotta' Shakin' Goin' On* or Del Shannon high-noting his way through *Runaway*.

Sometimes we got off the bus on Union Street and walked up Greaves Street heading for the half-moon-shaped car park situated where the Post Office now stands on Lord Street. Making our way through the car park we often saw a young woman, not very tall, in her early twenties with long black hair and the face of a movie star. She wore the tightest jeans she could possibly be poured into without circulation problems and dismounted her leopard-skin-seated Triumph Tiger Cub motorbike, hauling it onto its side stand without effort, considering that there wasn't much of her. We waited patiently while she took off her crash helmet and shook her long dark hair out; it flowed like a cascade down her back and swished softly on her leather jacket as she walked by. She was stunning, striding past us in her high-heeled, calf-fitted, knee-length boots and she never once glanced in our direction. It was great, there is nothing guaranteed to attract someone more than that person being totally ignored – well maybe good looks would do it or lots of money, owning a Pacific island or a pub... ah, never mind. She didn't turn up if it was raining though, so we didn't see her all that often come to think of it. I expect the girl enjoyed receiving the attention as much as we enjoyed giving it. A few minutes later, after much gabbling and wishing, we could be found standing or slouching, at Greenwood's drinks stall in the inside market. Around the late nineteen-fifties/early nineteen-sixties the stall was something of an institution for youngsters at weekends. I think the lad running it was called Rod and he bore a resemblance to Elvis, which was probably a plus for the business. Kids hung around the stall waiting for Saturday night to come around, talking about their dates and the possibilities to be found therein (That's a fancy way of describing big talk and hot air). Otherwise, there wasn't a great deal for teenagers to do in town on Saturday afternoons; the money might stretch to a Sarsaparilla in Joe's, the herb shop on George Street, or a drink of that kind and there was the Arcadia on Manchester Street situated in a row of shops between King Street and Market Place, a slot and pinball joint, the type where 'you puts your money in and tries for highest score'. Whatever its failings the Arcadia had the best, possibly the loudest jukebox in town which could be heard blasting out as far down Manchester Street as Crossbank Street – roughly on a level with where Sainsbury's was situated until recently. During the working week, those of our age who were stuck to their beds or weren't exchanging their labour for wages, frequented the Arcadia at some time or other during the day. The premises were almost directly opposite the Labour Exchange (Jobcentre), which is now the Magistrates Court car park. (Some of those lads with little enthusiasm for work had to be careful with their comings and goings). The loud noises howling from the Arcadia's jukebox during the week generally disturbed the office staff at the Labour Exchange and on occasion they complained to the Arcadia's owner. The town was in full employment in those days and the staff weren't overworked. The complainers probably whinged that the racket was preventing them from doing their nails, reading the paper, discussing the symmetrical arrangement of Marilyn Monroe's chest or they might have been just enjoying a doze. The Arcadia's owner, whose name I cannot remember, usually threw a deaf-un when the complaint came in. The Arcadia was renamed the Green Parrot sometime later, which is rather odd; the town wasn't exactly green parrot country in those days. The place was frequently a starting point for an evening's entertainment in the pubs if you'd been unable to arrange yourself a date. Consuming a vat full of ale was less desirable than trying to consume a whole girl during the course of an evening in the back row of the pictures.

Speaking of the word "date", in the vernacular, the preferred word when setting out to seek someone of the opposite sex to spend the evening with was "trapping". The obvious question is, Why? If you ask me that question today, it will only draw from me a similar blank look to the one it did then.

'Went dancin' at the Carlton in Rochdale last night.'

'Did ya trap off then?'

'Nah, they were all rough 'uns, I didn't fancy any of them, ther wer nowt worth trappin'.'

'That's bad. We went to Blackpool on a coach from work.'

'Did you trap then?'

'Yeah, it wer dead easy, there wer so much talent th' 'unchback 'a Notre-Dame would've got fixed up. My mate got fixed up with a girl from Bolton and took her home on the train.'

'Keen weren't he, wer he on a promise or summat?'

'Don't know about that, but he wer dead keen, when they got there he had no more money, so he kipped down in her dad's garden shed. He had to thumb his way home and only got back at ten o'clock this morning and he forgot to write down her address, the dozy sod.'

In daylight hours around the town, everyone was casually dressed; lads (without exception) wearing denim jeans with three to four-inch turn-ups. Apart from the normal-style denims (which we bought from Paulden's in Manchester) you could go to a stall at the top-end of Tommyfield Market on Saturdays where a stallholder would take measurements of your waist and inside-leg. The jeans would be ready for you in two weeks' time. The denims that this chap offered were known as 'drainpipes' because the trouser legs were the same width all the way down and tight fitting. They came with slash-cross pockets edged with red tape – or any colour you fancied. If you really wanted to make a fashion statement he would provide – at a little extra cost – the same colour of piping down the outside of each trouser leg. Young lads milling about the stall wearing these haute-couture items resembled a flock of storks with cold legs and varicose vein problems. The jeans were such a tight fit, the flesh displacement added a couple of inches to your neck size. If there was a problem with the market jeans, it was their zips. The fashion had just changed from button flies to zips and the zips weren't of a robust nature. Unfortunately, youth enjoys sudden bursts of energy – however much it tries to conceal it – and likes to dash about now and again. Often, the only protest open to a tautly-stretched zip was to jump its tracks. There is nothing more wonderfully embarrassing than a busted zip on a pair of jeans, on a loud teenager, on a sunny Saturday afternoon, in Curzon Street Oldham, when his only other outer garment is a waist length denim jacket. Not funny for the occupant of the jeans, but a near-death experience in laughter for his mates. An occasion I recall made normal breathing so difficult that we all had to sit down on the flags outside Halon's shirt shop frontage while we recovered and planned our next move. There isn't one really except, while mobile, put your hands in both front pockets forcing them together and then stare straight ahead, or walk in the middle of a group, ready to dash into the nearest shop doorway if you spot a female of your acquaintance, oh, and don't climb stairs – anywhere.

Male youth in my time had many leftover tribal instincts deep in its psyche and some items were worn with a bow to uniformity. Should an Alpha youth appear wearing a daffodil on top of his head you could soon expect to see the teen-field full of narcissi – that type of thing. Most lads wore denim jackets to complement their jeans; short, zipper-type leather jackets were an expensive option and much coveted. (The full-drape, piped-edge, knee-length jacket of the Teddy Boy was on its way to the rag recyclers by then). Upper-body wear was usually an ordinary shirt with a white tee shirt underneath it (oddly some lads wore pink shirts – not exactly a hard-case colour for those days). Dress shirts had flyaway or cut-away collars, the collars being permanently turned upwards when not covering a tie, thus placing the collar points somewhere around the jaw. The two shirt buttons nearest to the collar were left undone, often revealing a fine gold chain around the neck. Displayed on the chain against the tee shirt might be a small coin medallion, St. Christopher medal or a crucifix, depending on your decorative or religious leanings. Some lads wore bootlace ties; the tie's presentation dictated the addition of a metal toggle to draw the two sides together at the throat. Toggles came in whichever style you fancied or could 'acquire' (bulls' skulls, skull and crossbones, policeman's tunic badge, Iron Crosses, silver dollars, flattened jam-pot lid, whatever). When I first came across this method of holding your shirt neck closed I wasn't an admirer, preferring the usual type of tie because they looked better. Bootlace ties looked suspiciously like a garrotte to me. (I'm a suspicious person. I remember well the day that I got married; the vicar smiled throughout the proceedings – how suspicious is that?) Should a very angry man – whom you've offended – be stood in front of you and intent upon damaging your head, why wear that type of neck decoration thereby giving him the excuse to grab the laces and try to remove your head completely? Rubber-soled, wedge shoes were in fashion during that time, probably owing to connivance between the manufacturers and the Council's street cleansing department. They were low-profile shoes and in the habit of picking up discarded chewing gum, which in turn collected used matches, old bus tickets, cigarette ends and various unwanted bits of the catering trade. Some of the lads, with a higher level of sophistication than the rest of us, wore blue or black suede shoes with large silver buckles and crepe soles; the latter component announcing your arrival on wet floors by emitting loud sucking and squelching noises. The delicate quality of brushed suede was the only drawback to those shoes; it meant that you couldn't go out if it was raining. If a lad stood accused of owning more than one pair of shoes, either his parents were affluent or he'd "borrowed" them. Lads who weren't happy wearing the footwear that I've just described wore

Italian-style winkle-pickers. *Those* shoes I wouldn't wear under any circumstances. They were extremely narrow in the fit, were excruciating to wear and after a short period of time the long pointed toes turned irreversibly skywards, giving the shoes a Chinese-slipper look. White socks were more or less obligatory – a few lads wore pink, lime-green and electric-blue or other pastel shades of hosiery, but they were lads usually inclined towards exhibitionism. The outfit was usually finished off with a broad leather belt, the ends of which were held together by a large, round, highly polished, brass horse-harness buckle or some foundry-made creation weighing a couple of pounds. Lads with sturdy legs filled the leather part of the belt with shiny studs or rivets – highly polished of course.

Some of those belt buckles were sharpened and the belts used as weapons in the internecine battles that were fought out periodically behind the Savoy Dancehall. With regard to the attire worn by the town's male youth as they strutted their stuff on Saturday afternoons, ensembles often looked as if Andy Warhol and his mates had attacked them in a paint store while under the influence of the coca plant residue.

During those Saturday afternoon meetings at the drinks stall, some of the girls arrived with their hair in curlers in preparation for the night's entertainment. The curlers were hidden under a semi-transparent, pink chiffon-type headscarf. The girls nearly always wore full war paint, giving a Venetian facemask type appearance. Why is it that women are deemed to be more attractive with shades of pink, blue and bruised plum dotted about their faces, whereas if a man turns up with a face of the same colouring after a bout of contention, they would look at him as if he were a gargoyle or something similar? Whatever else girls wore as ordinary daywear, apart from the obligatory flared skirt, was usually hidden under a 'shorty' lightweight raincoat; the general effect was rounded off with a pair of black ballerina pumps. Many older women displayed a willingness to disport a skilfully turned curler or two during the day. It's a peculiarity of the human condition that thinks that at 2.30p.m. a woman can parade around town with her hair set like rows of sausages under a fishing net and then turn up in the pub at night, in front of the same people she has seen about town, with hair like an undulating cascade of burnished silk. Perhaps a decent coiffure at night made a difference to the taste of the alcohol. Some of the girls gave the more observant amongst us a peek at how things might turn out in time to come, if one were to be married to them. I suppose a measure of your expectancy for any future arrangements could be gauged thus – if they didn't look too bad when in this condition they would probably do for the long haul. (I never had a girlfriend who participated in those Saturday afternoon meetings). When the girls turned up for your combined evening's entertainment they usually looked like beautifully turned-out Ferraris. It was amazing, the transformation from plain scone to a good wedge of chocolate gateau. Again, a large wad of chewing gum was a major part of the girl's overall presentation.

Everyone chewed gum in those days, including adults. Some people – girls particularly – turned the practice into an art form. Three or four girls standing together might treat you to the sight of communal bubble blowing while they were talking. They might indulge in some synchronised chewing or pulling long strands from their mouths and sucking it back in – as you would with strands of spaghetti – if the conversation was running a bit dry. A friend of mine told me that he went out with a girl who would chew gum while they were kissing, changing the gum from one cheek to the other without breaking contact. Nothing like a bit of professional masticating as a method for creating awe and adoration in the one you love. After a few hours of oral contentment, the 'chewy' started to take on some of the characteristics and flavour of a bicycle's inner tube. Flattening it with your tongue and placing it in front of your teeth permitted the gum to make a satisfactory popping noise when you tried to suck air through it and into your mouth. A deal of skill was required though because an over-enthusiastic suck could result in an embarrassing, near fatal choking fit if the gum wedged itself in your windpipe. It was also inadvisable to fall asleep before removing the gum from your mouth as it usually slipped out of your snoring mouth during the night and would cement your hair to the pillow. Having to cut your hair free in the morning meant having to explain to friends why you had suddenly developed a bald patch. There were two types of gum available, bubble gum which was pink and capable of being inflated into football-sized bubbles when it was still fresh and white gum which you could buy from machine dispensers, usually in the form of white tablets – four to a pack. Popular makes were P.K., Chix and Wrigley's. One of those firms – I can't recall which – made coloured, fruit-flavoured tablets later on. The most coveted and expensive was Wrigley's Spearmint Gum which came in long strips – five or six to the pack. When I was very young, if I was lucky enough to come across a new strip of that brand, I could make it last three days without any problem. If you had a drink of hot coffee or tea when the chewing gum was nearing the end of its use, the gum became reconstituted and very sticky. Trying to throw the stuff away afterwards was like trying to throw away a ferret that had a hold on your finger.

The Saturday afternoon meetings at Greenwood's generally broke up as the sun was beginning to throw long shadows across the town, or if people had to join a queue at home before they could have a hot bath in readiness for the night's activities. If you stayed a little over departure time or perhaps went into Woolworth's to admire yourself in the large mirrors near the shop's exit doors, you would hear a sound not usually heard south of Werneth. Standing behind a low wooden box at the bottom of Curzon Street, in one of the loudest voice you're likely to hear, a short man wearing baggy trousers, an oversized raincoat, a square foot or so of weathered skin and round-rimmed National Health spectacles would be shouting, 'Hreen Fyniw", 'Het yer Hreen Fyniw niow' 'Fynaw sores, Het your Hreen Fyniw niow' which translates into: 'Green Final, Get your Green Final now, final scores, get your Green Final now'. Of course you knew that didn't you? He was the man selling the *Oldham Evening Chronicle*'s Saturday sports supplement – printed on green newsprint and sometimes the words were smeared or a bit blotchy, probably in the newspaper staff's hurry to get copy onto the streets. The weekly issue was produced on the same size of page, or near enough, to the *Chronicle*. The *Manchester Evening News* had a similar supplement termed the *Pink Final*. I can't recall whether anyone mangled the salesman's pitch for that item. The town was full of public shouters at the time; the man I've just mentioned must have had a brother or someone who studied under the same tutor as he. That chap stood at the junction of Watersheddings Street and Counthill Road late on Saturday afternoon shouting exactly the same thing, as spectators were leaving the ground of Oldham Rugby Football Club after a home game. Neither of them however, was in the same class as a small chap who trundled a wooden box, which used cast iron clothes-mangle drive wheels and two long wooden shafts for the vehicle's handles. The man was perhaps five feet two inches in height and whippet thin; his voice was of bugle quality and could be heard for miles. While walking the streets, he shouted 'Nyol' Raaa's – Cree' sones' which translates into 'Any old rags – Cream Stones', the latter being a sandy block of some composition or other used to "stone" the front doorsteps of houses in order to brighten up the streets a bit. The same ragman could be seen drinking around town on Saturday nights in a good-quality black suit with accompanying dickey-bow. It wouldn't have surprised me if he'd had a Bentley or a Maserati tucked away in a side street somewhere nearby.

I'm informed that occasionally, when the Arcadia youth co-operative found itself with nothing to do during the week, gang fights were arranged with lads from the Roxy Milk Bar – who didn't always turn up for the chest thumping dos. It's likely that being short-handed meant a Pow-Wow along the lines of 'There isn't enough of us, so sod it we'll do somethin' else'. When there was enough cavalry available, the venue was Jackson Pit, which was a croft behind Manchester Street and King Street. There were no rules associated with those primitive bouts of chest thumping and being a group activity, a variety of aids could be employed, bicycle chains, knuckle-dusters, pieces of iron railing, the odd bottle, anything to hand really. The police were not invited of course, which is perhaps as well, one or two of them were happy to join in such altercations. Magistrates in those days often had the dubious pleasure of looking down upon battered faces.

'What *have* you done to your face young man?'

'It was the coppers wot done it, your 'onourable, worshipfulness, sir.'

'Constable, have you anything to say by way of explaining the condition of the defendant's countenance.'

'We had to subdue the defendants before we could arrest them, they were a lively lot, sir – and we 'aven't got a punch bag in the new police gymnasium yet.'

There was the odd character with a darker side to their violent inclinations; they carried flick-knives or cut-throat razors. Flick-knives had a spring-loaded blade that opened when a small lever was lifted at the blade's pivot. Pressing the lever closed after the blade was in place locked the blade up in the open position. The knives usually had a crossbar at the base of the handle to stop the hand from sliding onto the blade when the knife was in use. When the knife was in its position of purpose, it resembled a stiletto. (Ownership of the knives was forbidden by law, so naturally most lads wanted one). They were quite often a point for discussion.

First lad to his pal Rupert walking up Henshaw Street, hands in pockets, looking at two older lads across the street:

'See 'im over there.'

'Who?'

' 'im with a face like a busted clock.'

'Which one of them?'

' 'im with loads of tattoos an' full 'a spots.'

'Oh, him. What about him?'

''e's gorra flick-knife an' he uses it, 'e 'as 'onest – ask 'im?'

'Get lost, you ask him'.

'I'm nor askin' 'im, no chance. Hey, can ya 'ear mi shoes squeakin'? Looks like rain again dun't it? A could murder a smoke, lend us a fag will ya? Wat wi doin' tonight then Rupe?'

Cut-throat razors were uncommon as a weapon. Those used as pocket fillers were usually taped up within a half inch from the business end or filed flat to the same length – you wouldn't want anybody to actually die, would you? The other bonus with the filed-down and taped versions was that "Dopy Dan" didn't cut his own fingers off while exhibiting his blade-closing skills prior to slipping the thing back into the top pocket of his jacket. You might have found the odd person carrying a set of knuckle-dusters; they were pretty fearsome-looking things, but if used incorrectly they busted the fingers of the user rather more than the head of the recipient.

Speaking of recipients, I was present at an incident where a Police Cadet (not cadetting of course at 10p.m.) agreed to enter into combat with another lad on waste ground at the back of the Savoy Dancehall. They both walked off into the darkness without speaking to each other about what the young cadet was about to receive. A lot of thumping, whacking and a good bit of swearing later, the lad walked back with a smile on his face. The lad smiled a lot; he honestly didn't look the type who would get involved in a fight or "a barney" as they were popularly known. Maybe his opponents thought the same thing. The lad could be a thoroughly respectable chap by now and have no wish to be associated with such undignified goings-on. I don't know what happened to the apprentice bobby except that he didn't come back from the fight. He could still be there for all I know. Bloodletting was treated almost casually in those days.

Some years later I associated with some blow-on-the-wind types, one of whom applied his predilections equally between extermination, brawling, drinking, vulgarity and womanising. The man pursued his pleasures with unrelenting enthusiasm and vigour. Unusually, he claimed to be devoutly religious and firmly believed in the after life. Personally, I think that one drunken night someone had told him that with all his shortcomings he would probably end up retired and stressed in Devon and he'd misheard that as 'admired and blessed in Heaven'.

7

In our early days about the town, before any of us ran off to do some serious courting or made failed attempts to get into prison, there was a period when as a group we were more or less still intact. There was the odd exception to that of course. One of our lads had been chosen for an evening's entertainment by a lady old enough to be his mother – say in her mid thirties. He fell foul (or lucky, if your morals are negotiable) of the woman when we had all been to investigate, for the one and only time, the doings of Saturday Night at the Savoy. She pounced on him, much as a nicotine-starved tramp dives on a discarded cigarette butt of more than an inch in length. The encounter ended up being a classic piece of dodgeridoo. Apparently after an educating grapple in the woman's kitchen with the lights out, he managed to dodge out of the back door of the house as her old man wobbled in through the front door. Our lad was mightily pleased with his good fortune and, on the last bus going home, gave a fair impression of what cockerels do first thing in the morning. We gathered shortly afterwards that he wasn't crowing much the next time he saw the lady. She told him that her husband was stoking-up his shotgun (metaphorically) and when he found out who it was that had been seen running out of their back door, he was going to blow large chunks of his anatomy into the following week and risk being the star attraction at a hanging. He never did – need to be hanged, I mean.

The favourite watering hole for most of the Savoy's youthful clientele was the Odd House pub, which stood opposite the top of Barker Street on Henshaw Street. It had a fairly good jukebox and the landlord was a pretty even type of bloke. The beer was made by Wilson's Breweries and well kept – meaning that it had the burnt-hop taste, a good head of froth and you didn't get the odd pint of vinegar that comes with unclean barrel pipes. On Saturday nights in the pub, if you were into a bit of stargazing, you would find Johnny Noon and maybe a couple of his team-mates from the Oldham Rugby Club having a relaxing pint after a match or training for the next match by quaffing a few more. There was one occasion, unconnected to the aforementioned rugby players as far as I knew, when we picked up a chap who was doing a bit of stargazing from the floor of the men's outside toilets in the back yard. Apparently, he didn't see the fist coming towards him which had "Duck Immediately" written all over it and he was particularly concerned about his broken tooth which we had found on the floor. After we'd given him back his souvenir of the event, he said, somewhat amusingly, that if he ever found the bloke who had caused his discomfort he was going to kill him. We laughed fit to pee; he should have done that first time round and saved himself a half-decent smile. Males did lie around the town for various reasons and in unusual attitudes of repose on Saturday nights around 11pm. Wet or dry, drunk or sober, bruised and busted, the floor clutched them to its bosom without prejudice. Next door to the Odd House was The Welcome pub, whose premises no one seemed to enter more than once. It was very difficult to get drunk in there because the landlord, allegedly, watered down his beer so much. You would need a bladder the size of a forty-gallon drum and pockets big enough to hold a gambler's overdraft, to get even tipsy in there. One barrel of beer was thought to last the pub a month. If I'm giving the impression that we were drinking all the time, that isn't the case. It was Saturday night and maybe two pints Monday and Wednesday nights. I would go for weeks without a drink of beer when courting – besides we just didn't have the money.

Looking for variation one night, we went to sample the delights of the Trap Inn on Barker Street. Delights usually consisted of a good jukebox, good beer and a decent dartboard. Having used up the dartboard's attractions we took our beer into the best room to play records on the jukebox. It was early evening and the pub was empty. Many Shadows and Elvis records later a few young women – a bit older than us – came in carrying their drinks and sat down on the other side of the room. Regular trips along the toilet trail are a requirement of those who drink beer in any quantity and we were up and down like the Midland Hotel's lift. When some of the young ladies went to use the toilet facilities, which were out in the pub's back yard along with the Gents, two of our group followed them (I wasn't one of them). Whether they had been encouraged to do so I never found out, some form of conversation had taken place and our lads returned to their seats. Before you could say, "I've spilled mi beer", some large building-site types were filling the doorway to our room looking particularly unhappy. Unknown to our couple of apprentice Casanovas, they were the ladies' husbands, boyfriends – maybe someone else's husbands, who knows – who had been playing darts in the taproom across the passageway and out of our sight. It was over very quickly (we were sixteen, they were the wrong side of twenty one) pugilism took place and sore heads were handed out. There was something about the Trap Inn that prevented us from going in for a while, or for that matter, a drink. I can't think what it was just now.

8

While I'm still in the Coldhurst area of the town, I've remembered a 'do' that we all attended. One Saturday night we were invited back to a girl's house after drinking hours in the pubs. She lived around Frankhill Street, somewhere at the top end of town and had been going out for a short while with one of the lads. When we arrived at her house, there was a party in half-swing. To achieve full swing they offered us a can of Party-Seven bitter beer, one can holds seven pints of watery ale. We'd just got snuggled up close to the beer can when the girl's dad, who was well oiled, asked us, and everyone else present, if we wanted to hear something that was banned for consumption by the public (that's exactly what he said). With that he produced, with a dignified flourish, a long-playing record he'd kept hidden behind his back. Not knowing what to expect, or caring for that matter, we all said 'Ay'.

Whichever tree you swing in now, it's very likely that a certain amount of rudeness or vulgarity would be a source of amusement to you in your mid-teens. If you were a girl, then giggle-worthy might cover it. If that wasn't the case then I apologise, thinking that you will read on regardless. The record the girl's father produced was titled A World Championship Crepitating Contest (the word crepitating used as a euphemism for wind-breaking). The contest was being held in Australia between an old English Lord and a large, hairy, Australian sheep shearer. The record went on – with sound effects – in a round by round commentary explaining the training methods of the contestants (Peas, Port, Garlic, Sherry and other combustibles). There were one or two people in the room who didn't seem particularly amused; we young folk thought it was jaw-achingly hilarious. There is less inhibition amongst youngsters than amongst adults with regard to vulgarity, that's for sure. Some time later, when the dust had settled and those who were miffed about the episode had pushed off home, we set off to walk home too. Passing around another large tin of beer that someone had found in the girl's kitchen, we pondered the frumpishness of our elders. Not for long though. After midnight, pondering is harmful to the youthful brain. There are much more beneficial things to do with the brain in the early hours, like telling porkies about your drinking capacity and exaggerating the depths of affection exhibited by your last girlfriend.

The Wakes-week fair was held at a couple of different venues in my youth, either on Cheapside or the outside market grounds. Where they put the market stalls to make room for the fair I don't know. As was often the case with young males seeking an evening's entertainment, a quantity of beer had to be consumed before courage could make an appearance. Once the sought-for state of bravado had been achieved it was just a matter of catching up with your loved one, or your mates, who would be knocking around somewhere on the fairground. Edible items were for sale there: candyfloss, ice cream and toffee apples or you could buy fish and chips or pies from the chip shop on Henshaw Street nearby. The latter delicacies would often be consumed by fairground-goers who drank; the nourishment would be pushing along the previously consumed beer slowly finding its way around their stomachs. If you were in the vicinity of any of the rides around 10-10.30p.m. it was advisable to stand back and review a few options if you hadn't been drinking. Lads leaving the Waltzers where the mixture was given a thoroughly good shaking, sometimes felt compelled to share their intake with the people who were standing on the walkways. Standing on the steps of the Waltzers wasn't a good idea either. Often those lads stood up just as the ride was about to come to a halt, thereby catching quite a few onlookers standing further back. A thoroughly disgusting state of affairs ensued, sometimes including fisticuffs, as you can imagine. The defiling of people's clothing was of little interest to the dismounting lads, as groups of onlookers scattered before them like marching pacifists when a car engine has backfired. At times the fairgrounds had take-on-all-comers boxing booths for those who were drunk or hadn't the same power of reasoning the rest of us enjoy. Fancy putting your pretty little, clean-shaven face on the line and risking a serious confrontation with some battered old pug that ate old clogs for breakfast and chewed fence nails between meals.

There was an occasion when a piece of wood and a few choice words gave us cause for hurried reflection. The cheekiest lad in our group had purchased three ring-throws on a stall, with the intention of winning one of the many watches on display. The watches were in the centre of the stall and were pedestal mounted at various heights and spacing. To acquire a watch you had to have the luck of Marilyn Monroe's boyfriend, the fingers of a safe-cracker, or own a loaded Browning automatic rifle in your earnest pursuit of a timepiece. Feeling a bit disgruntled when he didn't even hit the pedestal, our lad suggested to the lady in charge of the stall that the rings wouldn't fit over the pedestals anyway. The lady passed a ring up and down the pedestal and replied in some kind of guttural language, which we interpreted to mean 'Please go away'. By now our lad was showing signs of being gruntled and replied to her in kind. A very large rough-looking man, sporting a face like the aftermath of a train crash soon arrived and seemed to speak the same language as the lady. He was carrying something similar in size to the leg off a small kitchen table. Thinking about the future and our still needing one, we realised that there were many attractions that had yet to be sampled. By that time the table leg was beginning to look like a medium-sized piece of telephone pole, so we strolled away from the stall in a fairly nonchalant manner, telling him how handsome he looked and what a wonderful way with words he had. Don't believe me if you don't want to.

Once finished with the hard-man stuff, you could go and shoot small rifles at rows of moving metal ducks. The pastime had merit if you wanted to show any watching girls how you would fare when you came up against Robert Mitchum or some other cinema-screen hard case. The little .177 slugs that the rifles fired were gasping for breath by the time they reached their target. Some were so weak they were heard to say 'Excuse me', before falling out of the end of the rifle's barrel. The velocity of the pellets would possibly have caused concern to a wind-blown paper bag, although I doubt it. You'd need a lot of those pellets to make some of the Panatella-sized rounds I became friendly with, in the not-too-distant future (but that's another story).

There were some sorry drunken states wandering about the fairground at eleven o' clock at night, often with girlfriends in tow. It wasn't against the law to be drunk in charge of your girlfriend in those days, although it probably is today. There was one unspoken rule with regard to the fairgrounds and that was not to go upsetting the men who worked on them. Tough you may have thought you were, but you weren't even on the same planet as some of them. Fairground music would still be blaring across the town after midnight and could be heard from Mumps Bridge as we walked home towards the peace and quiet that was our village of Moorside.

Having spoken previously of ready-cooked food and some of its more distressing features, there was one occasion when I and my current young lady were bound, one fine Saturday evening, for the Gaumont cinema opposite the Star Inn on Union Street, Oldham. The lady had a change of mind *en route* and opted instead for the Grosvenor cinema on the corner of Peter Street and Union Street. We were-half way down George Street, which meant turning left on the next corner in the direction of the new venue. Completion of the manoeuvre brought us to the side or rear door of a recently opened Chinese restaurant called the Lung Wah. Passing the open back door of the premises we noticed that there were bread trays full of half-cooked chips spread out on the stone slabs of the outbuilding. Lying in magnificent splendour across one of the trays was a large black cat complete with sunhat and parasol, licking its fur with long relaxed strokes, eyes closed, purring contentedly and obviously relishing the moment. The animal stretched luxuriously as we watched the performance, unsheathing its claws in a manner more familiar in those of its much larger cousins. Yawning lazily, the cat gave us the benefit of a green-eyed stare before it returned to enjoying the early evening sunset whilst reading its Hemingway novel or doing *The Guardian* crossword puzzle. Presumably the creature was employed to terrorise any mice that misguidedly thought they could obtain a tasty, evening meal, very much as the restaurant's customers would soon be doing. Perhaps the cat liked a mouse and chips supper, or maybe it was just practising being a chip on the old block. Ever since that episode, Chinese restaurants have been places you won't find me in – I have no wish to offend any restaurateurs who may be reading this book and apologise if I do.

Mealtimes in those days were a pastime that featured way down the list of things-to-look-forward-to. In working families, certain hot meals tended to be served on the same day each week. Those who wished to protest about the monotony of the meal, were usually offered a scorching look accompanied by the phrase 'Get it eaten, it'll stick to your ribs'. The phrase was trotted out regularly, particularly if any child showed a marked reluctance towards getting its ribs sticky. (The observer never added that eventually it would stick to your stomach, backside and various components of your internal engine).

Nourishment in those days often meant a variety of cheap meat cuts, wormy potatoes and multi-coloured items grown on an allotment that had all been mashed together. These were consumed in much the same manner as breathing and your Saturday odd-money, you accepted them as a necessity for living. I was sitting in a short-term girlfriend's house one Saturday around teatime, in the company of her aunt while we were awaiting nourishment. This was long before vegetarians or Vegans came out of the closet. (I understand that Planet Vega is in the constellation of Lyra, in the vicinity of Outer Tune). The aunt was something of a large presence and dominated the room, sitting near to the windows and preventing quite a bit of daylight from getting through. From the look of her, not much food had managed to get past her during her lifetime. Eventually, after a few polite stabs at light conversation, we all became seated around the family dining table and began to explore the evening meal. It was to be the first and – as it turned out – the last opportunity for the girl's parents to inspect my table manners.

Without any prompting, the aunt said, 'I don't usually like eating meat, but I don't mind chicken as long as I pretend that it's lettuce'. Chewing this over I glanced across to my girlfriend's Dad, who was busy exercising his predatory instincts by harassing a few rebellious peas around the perimeter of his plate. Every time he stabbed at them with his fork, the peas sidestepped and headed for the sanctuary of the far side of the plate. Halting the chase, he stared vacantly at the aunt who was attacking her roast lettuce. The vacant sign on his face was soon replaced by an award-winning smirk. During that transitional process his eyebrows had managed to climb halfway up his forehead. He spent the next few minutes of the meal, glancing across the table at me, using a boring motion at the side of his head to indicate that he thought she was loopy. There was a degree of difficulty in not laughing at his antics, particularly when he was still holding his dining fork. He either lost concentration or the fork took on a life of its own, whatever happened, it made an unexpected move and jabbed him in the head. The unscheduled ill treatment of his temple made him yelp, releasing some half-chewed sustenance in a gentle arc, catching the cruet set and the corner of a plate of buttered bread. There followed a speculative silence as he did a bit of dramatic choking; the throat-tearing noise only stopping when his eyes were full to the brim with tears and he was getting short of breath. For a short while after the initial explosion he was reduced to embarrassing spasms of coughing. A period of high-pitched babbling followed the end of the eruption along with some chair-utching and beverage pouring. During one of those I sought the bathroom, which was upstairs, and therefore those assembled couldn't hear me laughing.

The aunt hadn't smiled when she fired the opening salvo, which made me think that white-coated attendants had brought her in a van.

Concentrated knife and fork work was in progress on my return to the table, while everyone digested the aunt's original snippet of information along with their food.

Later in the evening at the cinema, I had an image of the girl's aunt feeding carrot-shaped pieces of meat to her dog and I burst out laughing again – we were kissing and heavily entangled on the back row seats at the time. The unscheduled break in our common purpose was not very well received. Apparently it's reasonable to come up for air when transferring lipstick from one person to the other, but involuntary, raucous, disengagement is viewed with suspicion.

'You laughing at me then?'

'No, No, Wouldn't dream of it love'.

'What then?'

'Er nothing, can I get you an ice-cream or some Butterkist before the rush starts?'

'I'll have a large orange juice, a large Butterkist, a big bag of peanuts and a large pack of toffees.'

'That means I'll have to go to the kiosk in the foyer'.

'Well?'

Further speech wasn't forthcoming, the film suddenly became very interesting and later I had to walk home because the cinema kiosk had swallowed my bus fare. I walked her home first of course, damage limitation being my priority.

I can't say that I've ever been overly fond of vegetables in my time. Things were quite frosty with the girl for a while, which is unusual in late summer – even in Oldham.

Strange as it may seem, your style of haircut was the first indication of your standing in youth's community of disruption and surliness, especially those who sought stardom amongst their peers. Methods of attaining the desired coiffure were many and varied, but you can be sure that anything achieved with the aid of rollers, setting lotion, or your sister, was asking for it if you were ever found out. I found that the best way to subdue any hairs likely to be rebellious, was to wash my hair and towel it half dry, immediately adding whatever my thing in hair-cream was at the time. Depending upon my financial situation the product would be Brylcreem or Vitalis. If things were bad I'd use any kind of reasonable-smelling grease that was lying around on our Jean's dressing table. I've used petroleum jelly or smeared a hard bar of Palmolive soap across my damp hair at a pinch; you only have problems with the latter if it rains heavily. A variety of hairstyles was employed in an effort to keep the ladies interested. The traditional Elvis style was worn by those with thick, dark hair and enough income to support the gallons of hair cream required to keep it in place. Some lads still affected the crew cut, which had refined itself to the edge of extinction and was returning to America from whence it came. There was also a peculiar style, the need for which I've never been able to fathom; its main characteristics took the form of a badly groomed hedgehog. All the hair was swept backwards and buried under a liberal coating of greasy stick-it-down except for a tuft above the forehead which was about an inch long, two inches wide and pulled forward to hang over the eyes resembling a bunch of escaped bristles from an old yard-brush. Both sides of the rest of the arrangement met at the back of the head culminating in what was known as a D.A. (duck's bottom), a vertical crease where the two sides of head hair met in the middle. I recall the screen actor Tony Curtis being liberally represented amongst our male film-going fraternity who wanted to extend their persona by sporting a hairstyle as near to his as possible. The production was similar to the previous creation, the difference being the floppy bit at the front, which on Mr. Curtis's head came in the shape of two half-tubes of hair meeting in the middle to form a 'vee-shaped' funnel and then drooping to the middle of the forehead. When days were sunny, wind-free and rainless, the style worked pretty well; when that criterion wasn't met – you'll have seen discarded tagliatelli… One other shortcoming of the style was apparent if the wearer happened to be a cigarette smoker. Cigarette lighters were fuelled with petrol at the time, the flame coming to life with sparks igniting a wick; the flames were notoriously fickle about the size they wished to attain on any given day. Newly fuelled petrol lighters were prone to bouts of exhibitionism. If it was over-filled, the whole lighter sometimes ignited, producing that rarely practised routine of the dancing classes known as the Hot-hands Shuffle. When the flames fancied a piece of you, your cute little Tony Curtis flop-over could easily be turned into a quarter inch of knurled stubble, backed-up defensively against your hairline. I was present on one such occasion in the gents' toilet at the Savoy and heard a fairly good whinge from a lad who had been nurturing the style for a couple of years. He said, 'I wer fed up with mi Tony Curtis 'aircut, 'e's a puff that bloke – a bloody big tart'. The lad was known to spend more than the usual amount of toilet-time combing his floppy locks. We all stood surveying the wreckage at the front of his head, which was pretty critical. He'd been observing his forehead in the small mirror at the end of the urinal as I walked in on the character assassination of his idol. The urge to smirk had to be firmly controlled on blesséd occasions such as that. After the unscheduled bout of singeing and in a somewhat aggrieved manner he said with a half smile, 'Bloody barber won't be getting his full money next time I go'. If he'd said that to *my* bloody barber he'd have found out that scissors have other uses besides cutting hair. Personally I wouldn't venture beyond a Ricky Nelson facsimile, with ear-lobe-length sideburns and the regulation D.A. For my monthly pruning I used the barber's establishment on the right-hand side of Henshaw Street, in the then new block of shops just before Burnley Street. The business was named Holroyd Hairdressers and was operated by two brothers; I think they lived around the Watersheddings area. When I first met the taller of the two men who would be responsible for my tonsorial presentation in the foreseeable future, he walked around me, much as an archaeologist might do when inspecting a newly-found mummy and after a little thought said 'Square neck is it, don't touch the sideburns, not too much off the top – *easy on the grease*?'

We got on famously from then on.

Recently I went into a hairdresser's shop in Bristol to get a trim prior to a wedding in my wife's family. I'd just had a humour-free row with a traffic warden and wasn't chuffed – as you might expect under the circumstances. I was sitting in the barber's chair while waiting to be attended to and looking at the familiar face staring back at me in the mirror. I could see that his face was set and looked like the contents of a rat-catcher's satchel. After a few minutes this hairdressing chap walked across to me wearing a baggy blouse, a pair of cord trousers, something similar to South African veldt-schöen on his feet, a wrist watch the size of a soup plate and hair as long as my mother's.

'What would you like sir?' he asked.

You know how it is; sometimes you want to say something uncouth like, 'To smack your little pink face with the front end of a very large truck'.

Knowing he wouldn't be pleased with that and might cry, I said, 'A Lamborghini'.

The chap looked somewhat unnerved and stuttered for a while; which resembled the noise that a pleasure boat makes when it is setting off on a park lake.

When the spluttering ceased, he said, 'Pardon me?'

Perhaps he thought I was asking for a cocktail or a new continental hairstyle.

I said, 'Never mind, just give it a trim' and settled back comfortably in the barber's chair.

He was nonplussed about that and seemed a bit edgy as he swished his scissors in the air, reminding me of a swordsman taking a few practice swipes at a tuft of grass. Feeling considerably better about life now that I'd sorted him out, I watched him suspiciously as he gave me the trim that I'd gone into the shop for. A fine job he made of it too. I didn't get off lightly though. With the amount of money he charged me for the service, he probably had three months' holiday in Japan, or bought himself an ocean-going yacht. I wouldn't have been bothered but quite a lot of my hair has had a serious disagreement with my head, setting off for pastures new some time ago. It's today's shampoo that does it of course; not as good as the stodgy stuff my mother used to ladle onto mine and my sister's heads, rubbing it in until our scalps tingled like a bad nettle rash.

Tattoos, usually displayed on the backs of the hands or the arms were worn as a sign of the wearer's uncompromising outlook on life and to let all and sundry know that he wasn't to be messed with. If you owned a few tattoos below the shirt cuff, I suppose you wouldn't need to wash your hands so often, because the dirt wouldn't show the same. Those extra adornments were often a personal design and laboriously imprinted with copy-ink and a sewing needle; a current girlfriend's name, tattooed in a scroll on the arm was most favoured amongst the cognoscenti. One lad had the words "cut here" with accompanying stitch marks tattooed on his throat. (In my early twenties I ran with a bunch of men who would happily have obliged him). I never knew what happened when the Romeo types ran out of arm space; perhaps they started on the legs. There must have been little comprehension about the meaning of some words amongst the tattooed ranks. Take the late-night taproom scufflers as an example. Many of them had "Love" and "Hate" tattooed across their knuckles. Some of these characters spent half their life punching the lights out of other men – you'd have difficulty convincing me that a face full of Love-knuckle was a message of affection.

I didn't have a tattoo; I had enough natural disfigurements to be going on with.

9

There were many times when you and your date spent Saturday night at the pictures and her facial masterpiece came out of the cinema looking a lot different than it had when it first walked in. The lengthy amount of time your girl spent painting her face in front of a bedroom mirror could be wiped out in two and a half hours of enthusiastic close quarter combat on the back-row seats of your chosen cinema. Smudging was a condition that occurred with some of the face improvers of the time. Lads had to hope that the girls hadn't bought cheap make-up, suit and shirt collars suffered if that was the case. In the cold, bright lights outside cinemas there would be revealed some strange results after a heavy bout of "necking", the girl's make-up having transferred itself to the lad. Quite a number of peculiar looking lads caught the last bus home. For some reason, maybe medical, a few lads looked pale and drawn, perhaps due to insufficient oxygen as they lengthily distracted their girlfriends who probably wanted to watch the film. I have heard of girls who were word perfect on the retelling of the plot of a film, even though their date had kept them occupied for great swathes of time during its showing. If your mouth is occupied and your eyes are shut, the ears still work, don't they?

Having taken your dishevelled date home and spent five minutes standing outside her front door while she straightened herself up for her father's inspection, you would begin wondering if the chip shop was still open. If it was, your supper consisted mainly of second-hand lipstick and chips.

I was reminded of this make-up phenomenon recently when I went to buy a Sunday newspaper from the newsagents in the village where I live now. As I approached the shop, two young ladies tottered out of a fairly beat-up old car, which they had parked opposite the shop door. They were obviously on their way home from some all-night festivities. Feeling gentlemanly and somewhat amused I waved the girls into the shop before me. Both girls wore high-heeled shoes and some form of nylon stocking. One of them wore what is best described as a Lycra scarf as her main means of body covering, the other wore a tight suit that parts of her body seemed to be trying to escape from. There were bits of blouse, brand name tags and other flimsy bits of construction hanging out all over the place.

They both stood teetering in front of the shop's counter while waiting for the old chap who owns the shop, to appear. They had a resigned air about them and did a fair amount of puffing and blowing in between slightly slurred conversation. One indicated to the other that they might be in for a bit of shouting-at when they arrived at wherever they where going. A smattering of multi-coloured eye make-up had transferred itself onto their cheeks and one of them had recently applied some lipstick with a good quarter-inch overlap onto her skin, made worse because it was a robust shade of purple. Some of the hair above one of that girl's ears looked decidedly bristly and threatening. I can't remember the quantity required or which type of alcohol does that to your hair – maybe it's tequila. (I have a faint recollection that slumbering in a puddle of the stuff, on a bar room floor in hot, malaria-producing climes produced that effect).

The old chap popped out of his hole eventually and stood looking at them for a few seconds with his head slightly inclined to one side. The girls waited for the start-gun that produces speech, still swaying lightly to and fro, their faces resembling those of a pair of inquisitive lemurs. The Lycra girl mumbled something about a newspaper for her dad. After an enquiring look in my direction at which I just shrugged, the shopkeeper asked which newspaper that would be. She said and I quote *ad verbatim*,' 'E likes the one wiv bare wimmin inside an' the footy results. Hoo, 'e in't 'alf gonna shout when we get in'. While offering that wisdom she carried on with her waving-cornfield stance, not missing a beat. The other girl stood at the side of her in similar mode, sagging now and again before righting herself. He pointed to the newspapers and said that any of those with red tops would fit her needs. A lot of raking about on the shelf and then in her purse occurred before she came up with the amount of money the man had asked her for in return for the newspaper. The girls turned as if at some unspoken instruction and wobbled out of the door, which I held open for them. Lycra scarf said 'Fanks' in my general direction as they walked through. They spent a further five minutes familiarising themselves with the inside of their car before driving off, peering through the windscreen like a couple of lost zombies. One of them turned her tired, streaked, but otherwise pretty face in my direction and waved at me as I walked along the pavement, offering what probably passes at any other time for a smile.

10

According to an accredited source in brewery circles, around the years 1959-60 the Chancellor of the Exchequer put a large historical stain on his character by reducing the tax on a pint of draught beer by two old pennies. It was a moment of thoughtlessness that the Inland Revenue Department never repeated again. The male drinking population of the British Isles became quite excited and got itself into a euphoric frame of mind on account of the government of the day's largesse. Observing the scenes of ecstasy that they had brought about and wishing to capitalize upon the great good fortune it had visited upon the masses, the government looked around the world for a country to start a squabble with. Unable to find one that it wasn't already at loggerheads with and not wishing to participate fully in the budding Vietnam conflict, they joined the rest of the country in picking a fight by proxy with the World Heavyweight Boxing Champion of that time, an American chap named Floyd Patterson. After running around the country looking for a likely candidate and doing a bit of fiscal bartering with various people the fight promoters narrowed the field down to a large and vociferous pugilist named Brian London of Blackpool, assuring him that he was the man to put Mr. Patterson straight about a few things. Alas, after eleven rounds or so of sticking his chin in front of every punch that Mr. Patterson threw at him, our Brian glanced at the ringside clock and began thinking that the comfort of his bed would soon be in the offing. Mr. Patterson, a thoroughly decent and obliging chap, duly accommodated our man by switching his lights out immediately, putting an end to his public chastisement. Brian lived in the dark for a few seconds after that. The British fight followers, their enthusiasm for a bit of a punch-up somewhat blunted, returned to the more profitable pastime of drinking nine pints of beer for the price of eight while toasting the Chancellor and declaring him to be a decent chap.

In the late fifties to early sixties, Oldham boasted enough pubs to slake the thirst of the nation. Highly qualified drinkers such as coal delivery lads who finished their work at lunchtime felt the need to go and 'sink a few' along with such members of Her Majesty's Armed

Forces as could be spared from duty on dark continents. Soldiers often drank during the day while waiting to have a drink at night. Those practising exponents of midday social intercourse didn't often indulge themselves in drinking outside the walls of their chosen pub. When I asked an ex-school pal of mine, who had joined the junior army at sixteen and a half years of age, why this was so, he said, 'Firstly, outside is a long way from the bar and second it's a well-known fact that beer evaporates in hot sunny weather'.

I looked at him and laughed, thinking it wouldn't get much chance with him holding the pot.

'Nah, seriously it does and not only because of the heat; inside the pub you keep your beer close at hand, outside you put your pint on a window ledge or a wall and it evaporates – somebody else drinks it.'

At weekends the town-centre hostelries were full to bursting, both lunchtime and night. If you were a man who liked to be called "Alice" at the weekend, they were not the places you should seek out – very tough some of them. Middle-aged men, who had fought in the war and worked in the building industries or heavy engineering, weren't about to take any lip from kids such as us. (Today's lot think that a fair fight can only take place if the odds are ten lads onto one. A good kicking then has to take place on the unfortunate one in order to soften the leather of their £200 Rockport boots).

If you fancied a fight on Saturday night, then it was the place to be. Testosterone was the main ingredient of most of the beer brewed in those years. One wrong look or absent-minded stare in any pub, especially at our age, would often invite that precursor of trouble, 'What're you starin' at mate?'

You knew with some certainty that being matey wasn't what the questioner had in mind. Your options were pretty limited from then on. You spoke the word 'Nothing', if you could speak at all, in which case the indiscretion was usually forgotten – or you started punching the enquirer. Invariably, the inquisitor had a mate somewhere in the bar so you were on a hiding to nothing if you chose the latter. If a night in town was in your mind and you were susceptible to periods of staring vacantly, selecting footwear normally associated with sprinters was to be fully recommended.

When we started out on the short if convoluted road to adulthood, £1 Sterling would cover all of Saturday night's events and there was usually change left over. Saturday night began with our catching the seven o'clock bus from Moorside and alighting just before Mumps Bridge, which was regarded as being on the fringe of Oldham proper.

Mumps Bridge didn't have the benefit of a traffic roundabout in those days. Lees Road, Huddersfield Road, Rhodes Bank, Bell Street, Wallshaw Place and Brook Street all converged at roughly the same place under the single bridge. When I was about nine years of age, before the advent of traffic signals, peak traffic meant no more than thirty vehicles on the main roads at the same time. When those circumstances occurred at around 8.30a.m. and 4.30p.m. one traffic policeman created his own small roundabout under the bridge by standing on a yard square, one foot high, black and white striped wooden box, for the purpose of stopping oncoming traffic while directing opposing traffic along its chosen route. No matter that the logo painted on the bridge above the policeman's head said *Guinness Is Good For You*, you could drink the stuff until you floated away, the job carried a health risk, which my father did his best to implement. He was singularly adept at catching the side of the wooden box with the footrest of his motorbike, which had a sidecar attached. That happened on a couple of occasions when I was riding pillion; the second time he succeeded in dislodging the policeman from his perch. You may well ask how you do that. The road was umpteen feet wide at our point of passage, the policeman's helmet at least was conspicuous, being roughly eight foot from the ground and his white, knee-length smock was the whitest thing I've seen since Jimmy Tibbs climbed off the Big Dipper at Blackpool not long after an orphan-making beer session. My father had never shown any inclination to spend time in Oldham Royal Infirmary or any of Her Majesty's Prisons, he didn't drink and wasn't particularly peevish. He may have been thinking of the 16th century poet John Donne, who so aptly penned the line, *No man is an island, entire of itself* – although I doubt my father had ever heard of him. As far as I know he didn't have a grudge against policemen; in fact he had a few friends on the force – well, people he was friendly with. The constable's face was woefully uneven as he picked himself and his helmet from the floor – I'd never heard a policeman swear. Father stopped his motorbike instantly and dismounted, standing and watching the bobby rearrange his coat and dust himself down; he didn't volunteer assistance although I remember he straightened the box from its askew position. They exchanged words, but I couldn't hear what was being said from my seat on the bike's pillion. I like to think my father would have had a light spring to his step on his return to our bike. Perhaps he regarded the event as a risky game of skittles. I don't know if there were fine-ancial repercussions afterwards and didn't care much either, I was quite happy with the situation; while father was clouting the policeman's box he wasn't clouting me.

Whilst I'm on the subject of railway bridges, British Railways employed a precision instrument known as Bower Lane Bridge, which, when not being used to transport trains above the highway, pursued a secondary pastime in neatly shearing the tops off double-decker buses, costing life and causing serious injury in the process. The edifice was also pretty good at detaining lorries with ambitious loads. The bridge had hidden depths in the shape of a large concrete reinforcing block slung underneath it and not readily visible on the approaches to the bridge.

Ah, railway bridges! I was once confronted many years ago with an accident at the railway bridge in Middleton Junction at the bottom of Foxdenton Lane, Chadderton. Protruding from the narrow, arched tunnel was a half-loaded lorry; the other half of its load was lying in carefree, disproportionate mounds, all of it being medium-sized cardboard boxes. Viewed today, anywhere in the vicinity of the Tate Gallery, the display would have been easily capable of winning the award for "Best Rubbish Jumbled" more formally known as the Turner Prize. The driver of the vehicle and half a dozen customers from the Lark and Linnet public house a few yards away were trying to fit the boxes back into their former square on the lorry, the load resembled the pigeon holes at the rear of the reception desk in the Dorchester Hotel by the time they'd finished. I was sitting on my motorbike, which disqualified me from assisting them in their endeavours, far too strenuous an activity for the leather-clad – handy things are motorbikes.

I've become sidetracked. A hurried walk from the bus stop at Mumps Bridge, playing "chicken" whilst dodging traffic, we crossed Lees Road at the white-tiled frontage of the Gentlemen's Public Conveniences. Passing Buckley & Procter's store and skirting the small square on the Rhodes Bank side of the bridge, we arrived at the Salisbury Hotel, situated on the corner of either Railway Street or Coronation Street in Rhodes Bank. Dress for the evening was best suit, white shirt, plain pastel coloured cotton tie, "casuals" (shoes without laces) and white socks.

The pastel ties were a fad of the time and came with a piece of card along the top of which was stitched a one inch, many triangular pointed strip of cloth the same colour as the tie. The idea was to cut the card to fit the top pocket of your jacket, the strip of cloth protruding from the top appearing to be a matching handkerchief. Fine until you were walking through town with a girl you'd fancied for ages and a couple of empty-head pals came along and tugged the cloth, exposing the card insert. My pieces of card had a few girls' names and addresses on them, so that I would remember who had to be returned to where. One town centre chum, sick of having that happen to him, scrawled a rude command across the top of the card; not nice for an inquisitive girl to read and fairly enlightening for his mum, should she venture to peek in his pockets.

The Salisbury was already full of young people when we arrived and there was a fair amount of noise about the place. Trying to find somewhere to park your beer was difficult if you were late and acknowledgement of casual acquaintances was given courtesy of the briefest of nods. (Curiously, out of the dozens of lads in our form at school, only a couple of them progressed to the town-centre watering holes for their entertainment. Maybe the others had more sense). Most of the lads wore suits and utilised a variety of haircuts; the girls mainly wore flared skirts and fitted tops, some wore "frocks" and many girls had enough lacquer on their hair to paint a small dinghy. Cigarette smoke hung in layers from ceiling to floor. On reflection and contradictory, if you didn't smoke, you did. Everyone gathered in the long room on the right-hand side of the entrance door to the pub, feeding the jukebox while waiting for live entertainment to begin. The hall carpet behind the inner front door had a hole the size of a dustbin lid and the original white or cream painted ceiling was a peculiar shade of light brown. The pub was wallpapered throughout with a small, gold, *fleur de lys* pattern, overprinted onto a dark green background. Presumably the paper was dark so that the walls wouldn't need re-papering before the pub fell down. The bar was in the room on the left-hand side of the front door and smelled of old railway carriages or stale billiard halls. I recall that the bar-staff liked a little joke at our expense if trade was slack and they thought that we were under age. The charade went something like this.

'Three pints 'a mild, please.'

''Ow old *are* ya?'

'Eighteen.'

''Ow old's yer mate?'

'Same.'

''Ow old's yer other mate?'

'Same.'

'Ya don't look like triplets ter me.'

'Ha, Ha, Haa, we are 'onest – eighteen I mean.'

'Do ya want it in a glass?'

'Eh?'

'Der ya want water with it or just a straw?'

'Ha, Ha, Haa,'

'Wat ya laughin' at then?'

'A thought ya were jokin'.'

'A wos, that'll be two pound one an' sixpence.' (£2.07½p)

''Owww much?'

'Three shillin's an' sixpence.' (17½p)

'Is that fer one pint?'

'Nah, it's one an' tuppence (6p) a pint, ya berk. Look 'ere, if the coppers come in, go out ta t'toilets int'yard an' jump over t'yard gate.'

The pub was darkly mysterious to us newcomers. Some of its early-start customers were agreeably steeped by the time we arrived and sitting on wall seats half hidden in the smoke-laden gloom near the bar; they weren't above the odd comment like "wet-behind-the-ears", "does-your-mother-know-you're-out", or "don't fall into that pint or you might drown". In spite of all that ribbing we loved the place, this was the grown-up world and we had finally gained admittance. You carried your pint of beer into the concert room as if it was a cup full of gold dust – having slurped the top off it first. The pub's waiters didn't start their evening work until between seven thirty and eight o'clock. In the concert room the jukebox might be playing *Apache* by The Shadows and if it were the favoured record of the moment, the machine would be asked to play the tune continuously half-a-dozen times or more. Live entertainment began around eight o'clock and was usually provided by the same group, band, whatever you wish to call them. The jukebox was switched off while they performed their routine (more or less the same songs each week as I remember). They'd hammer out a few numbers for an hour or so and then take a beer-break.

There were always a couple of lads in the audience who would get up on stage without too much encouragement and give us a song – sometimes they needed a spoonful of beer to convince themselves of their talent, getting them to sit down again was sometimes a problem once the'd got the bit between their teeth – so to speak. I was amazed on my first introduction to these proceedings, to see an older lad from our village get up and give his rendition of the Elvis song *Blue Suede Shoes*, swiftly followed by an Eddy Cochran song entitled *Cut Across Shorty* which earned him a generous round of applause from the audience. The lad sang *Blue Suede Shoes* and *Cut Across Shorty* every Saturday night that we went into the pub – which is alright of course, all amateur singers stuck to what they knew, but the same songs can be something less than stimulating at times. Still, it was something that I wasn't about to do, even on the promise of free beer for life. Regardless of his limited repertoire we all liked him – he was a good bloke, always up for a laugh and the odd fight if the opportunity presented itself later in the evening. He was very popular with the ladies and at times had some real peaches in tow.

When he'd finished his songs, his age group of lads moved on to the Friendship Hotel further up Rhodes Bank. It was the most frequented young-people's pub in town at the time. Pubs seemed to be spaced every two hundred yards or so at the bottom end of town. Hardly had we left the music behind from one pub than we were enveloped in a rush of loud pounding music from the next one. We followed the older lads from one pub to the next at a respectful distance, no sense in provoking a stressful moment – those could be very painful even if the older lads were just being playful. Standing room let alone seating, was at a premium in The Friendship, none of the modern-day chatting in cool airy comfort, more a case of sweaty, sticky, shout-in-your-face discourse. Somewhere in amongst the press of bodies, a jukebox tried to crack the plaster on the walls, in its efforts to be heard. People sat on the stairs to get away from the noise, making it difficult to pass them to gain access upstairs. Getting a drink after nine o'clock was no mean feat. As if achieving that goal wasn't arduous enough, drinking the beer when you got it was equally difficult. Every surly male in those days worked on the principle that to spill beer was a sacrilege and became prayer-worthy if it ran down someone else's neck, shirt-front or his lady's dress-front. Dripping on people could be detrimental to your health and positively dangerous to your good looks, if you had any. The crush of bodies meant that there was at least one consolation when the pub was full – there wasn't much room to fight. Young people always want to fight about something or other. The cardinal rule of the day was, for the sake of economics, always drink your beer first and fight afterwards, that way you cut out any waste.

The Friendship Hotel had one thing going for it that other pubs in the locality didn't have, it had a girl magnet. Where they kept the attraction or what form it took I don't know. The place was awash with girls, most of them unattached and none of them interested in white-faced fifteen to sixteen-year-old lads. Hope rose in the midst of our eagerness each time we walked into the place and the casual search for a connecting glance was uppermost in our minds. Anticipation was soon replaced by apathy and irritation when the only interest was shown by girls who didn't fit the outline requirements that most of us have. I had a template from which any candidate had to have very dark hair, plenty of money, a pretty face, her figure had to be on the medium slim side and she should be the owner of the longest and shapeliest legs this side of a Queen Anne chair. (Not much of a requirement there then). It goes without saying that there weren't many girls around with such Hollywood attributes in those days; if there were they weren't bothering with me and they weren't in The Friendship on Saturday nights either. The template went out of the window fairly soon after those early forays.

The next pub on the itinerary was the Royal Oak at Rhodes Bank; music came from upstairs in the pub and was usually live. I can't remember what the interior was like; I think it was on the small side and dark, it wasn't as popular as the previously mentioned pubs and rarely merited our buying a drink there.

By this time in the evening, the beer would be encouraging us to throw caution to the winds. Along with that caution went any credibility amongst our mates if we were seen going into the Grey Horse on Union Street. The one time I can recall going to the pub – we ran all the way there, only stopping when we were outside the premises – the billboard in the doorway announced 'Tonight it's Renee On The Spoons'. (There you go that's the credibility side of things). Walking into the pub we were puzzled by the peculiar sounds we could hear coming from the big room. Having a gander through the doorway we found a nicely-proportioned lady in a tight dress standing in the middle of the room banging a couple of tablespoons enthusiastically on her well-shaped thigh, which produced a clacking noise in accompaniment to some tune or other. She smiled in greeting at us and winked lewdly (although she could have had smoke in her eye I suppose) inviting us to sit down near those windows overlooking Hobson Street. I recall Terry nearly collapsing with laughter at what we saw – laughter usually means a quick visit to the toilet for most lads after a few pints have been quaffed – he couldn't find the toilets and because of the noise the artist was making, couldn't hear the reply when he asked someone. I think it was a close run thing, with him just triumphing over his bladder when he eventually made contact with the gurgling trough. Good-looking the lady may have been, but as a form of entertainment this spoons thing was a bit of a bind, we being used to hearing steel guitars and huge *Vox* speakers bellowing forth. Had she been rhythmically banging someone's head on a table or a couple of snooker cues on her thigh, there may have been some novelty interest in what she was doing. We didn't invest in a pint of beer as far as I can remember; the entertainment apart, it was probably because the pub was full of older folk. After ogling the lady for a few more minutes we finally departed to go to the Stags Head pub on West Street. The entertainment there was very loud; it had to be to compete with the Top Drum pub at Market Place. The noise coming from the Stags could be heard half way down King Street and was produced by a piano. A well-rounded individual named Ronnie, who physically vibrated as he pounded the life out of its keys, encouraged the piano in its endeavours. Later in the evening he would shout at random while sweating buckets and staring wild-eyed at the ceiling, lost in the rapture of his playing. His pint glass moved around in little zippy movements on the top of the upright piano, sloshing beer around as if it were watering window boxes. When he'd finished drinking the remaining beer in his glass, someone brought him another pint and off he went again. I used to think that most of the customers were mill-workers, using lip reading as a means of communication. There was no possibility whatsoever of the normal methods of speech or hearing being employed, while Ronnie was at full throttle. One thing's for sure; if it wasn't their quota of beer that did it, clientele who stood anywhere near the piano were guaranteed a Town-Hall-sized headache the following morning. One pint of beer was all we would invest in at the Stags Head. The evening was heading in a downward direction by this time and your alcohol-impaired choices were the Top Drum – which required an amount of indifference to the normal human state – or the Regent Hotel, both at Market Place. Dr. Syntax pub was always empty and we steered clear of the Wine Lodge late at night for reasons unknown to me, maybe it was tales about the boisterous element who inhabited the Deep-end of the establishment (wherever that was). The Albion Hotel, next on the tour, required an even greater amount of indifference than did the Top Drum.

First though, to enter any of those hostelries, you had to get past Little Harry, known on the drinking circuit as "Rommel". When unencumbered by beer, Harry was a nice chap; he was a nice chap when he *was* cumbered and would tell anyone willing to listen that he was an ex-desert rat who fought alongside Field-Marshal Montgomery at El Alamein (the army having an order of pecking, Harry probably fought in front of him). If Harry was feeling empowered, he was defender of the traffic roundabout at Market Place. I was introduced to the town's late-night defences for the first time when I became aware of the simulated sound of heavy machine-gun fire being directed at traffic coming up West Street from Rochdale Road on Saturday night. Harry was manning his imaginary gun-pit on the island, mowing down anything that moved including the patrons of the Top Drum if they cared to emerge and change pubs. He occasionally turned his attention to the Regent Hotel customers if business was slack around West Street and Cheapside. Anyone thinking they might do a bit of quiet courting in Weston's doorway – a ladies' clothes shop on the corner of George Street and Market Place – was sadly mistaken if Harry was on picket duty. Had Harry been shooting for real, the Co-operative Undertakers on Union Street West would have had to strip the Amazon rainforests bare of wood over one weekend. Little Harry was a harmless and uncomplicated character. If he and Montgomery were ever comrades in arms, I like to think that the fact is recorded in Arabic, on the hot winds of the sirocco as they drift in veiled curtains across the North African deserts. The thought soothes and pleases the small amount of romance that resides within my soul.

We'd occasionally investigate the Market Hotel on Curzon Street for a change of scene. One of my later visits to this pub was with a friend, home on leave from the army. We got involved in a disagreement with a drunken chap who was being tedious with us. It was getting a bit late in the evening and the place was packed out. Some of the pub's customers (I nearly wrote "clientele") were suffering from serious facial cave-in and one or two were practising hiding their eyeballs in the roof of their skulls. Most of those who were still on the programme were red-faced and not particularly

76

animated as they spoke to the bar top, or shouted to the person next-but-three down. Others muttered contentious phrases to people that couldn't be seen, on the far side of the room – couldn't be seen because they weren't there. Others entertained themselves by quietly singing songs in a slurred manner, some of which were quite rude. We stood politely at the rear of the throng at the bar, waiting for a gap to open up so that we could be served. That didn't happen so we pushed our way in. The area of contention with our primeval friend was about our pushing him aside, which was only partly true. He was nudged a bit, which isn't the same thing. Cutting out the niceties, he was spoiling for trouble. The man looked to be in his thirties and was a bit of a lowbrow, the type you would take to the dentist to have a wisdom tooth put in. In my heightened condition I gave him that which he required, delivered by my hardest punch to his head. There was the loud crashing noise of a table in descent as we scuttled out of the door like two crabs passing a pan of boiling water. It was more than likely that the bloke had a few mates dotted around the place so prudence was called for. Scampering off towards High Street and then Yorkshire Street without waiting to see the full results of my unexpected action (unexpected by both him and me and certainly not expected by my mate who had just ordered two pints) we couldn't achieve great speed through laughing too much. At that time I harboured one or two ambitions in life; walking around with a face like a busted backyard gate wasn't one of them. I never rated John Wayne high on my list of role models. Although it's true I'd previously been involved in a few juvenile skirmishes, they were nothing that would make Lennox Lewis lose any sleep over. We collapsed on the steps of the Greaves Arms and laughed until I got hiccoughs, keeping one eye open for pursuers, of course. As luck would have it, none appeared.

That wasn't the real reason for our good humour. The light-weight, hand-made suit that I was wearing was not a cheap one: a beautifully cut, link-button jacket at just less than fingertip length with narrow hand-stitched lapels and lightly padded shoulders, a full-drape back with a single vent. The trousers were finely tapered with slot cross pockets, 12-inch bottoms and no turn-ups. The material was fine wool worsted and a dark shade of lovat green.

(It was a wonderful piece of equipment considering that my father's age group were still wearing gangster, pin-striped, double-breasted jackets with barn-door shoulder pads and 22-inch bottomed trousers with 2-inch turn-ups. In a tight corner, men of my father's age could take hostages and hide them inside their suits – whilst they were still wearing them).

My outfit was refined and unaccustomed to moving at the speed it was being asked to at the present time. The only time it had moved any faster was on a bus and eventually my trousers decided to go public in their distress. A seam in the crotch split from the bottom of the fly almost to the rear waistband, which proved somewhat unfortunate for me. The dress code of the time forbade the use of underwear in young men – never mind what your mother said about wearing clean underwear in case you were knocked down by a truck and the ambulance staff suffering trauma at your lack of suitable under-garments, or hospital nurses having an attack of the vapours due to your semi-nakedness upon your gory arrival at the front door of the hospital premises. Walking the two miles home as if I was knock-kneed was quite difficult. If my legs bend at all they bend the other way and I didn't dare get on a bus. I gave the Market Hotel a miss for a while after that.

The Albion public house at the bottom of Curzon Street was a dire place to spend time in. I have no wish to upset anyone who once frequented the downstairs part of the pub with my observations, but if I do upset them then either they were sight-impaired or I was. The bar area was heaving with bodies, the customers twisting and wriggling like worms in a bean-can and the noise was way, way above the decibel limits of ordinary people. The roar was similar to the noise emitted by a fighter plane when the pilot has lit-up his aircraft's after-burners, an occasional top C shriek gave the room a much more human quality. From what I could see of it, the only way they could communicate was by shouting into each other's faces. Gawd, it was rough! Two policemen stood outside the pub from 10p.m. onwards just in case – the case was usually proven. Upstairs in the pub you could buy only bottled beer, no draught beer, and you weren't allowed to be clever by purchasing a pint downstairs and taking it up with you. At weekends an artiste named Benny sang a few songs to relieve the boredom. He was slim, wore glasses and his suits always seemed a size too big for him. He could be relied upon to entertain you (I use the word 'entertain' without seeking a true definition) until the beer got to his Plimsoll line and he had to retire gracefully. That's hearsay; we only went into the pub a couple of times and only stayed a short while. The only common denominator between Benny and Elvis was that they were both wrapped in skin. I'm not altogether sure when I used the word 'gracefully', if that was the case either. Closing time would be approaching around then and we usually started to head for home five minutes before the landlord called 'time'. Hardcases in the town set out looking for trouble and had often found it by fifteen minutes after closing time. Ample policemen were on duty and were amply built to handle the trouble without any kind of involvement from the likes of us. I know that some of those policemen would take the Saturday night stint because of the likelihood of trouble – not in spite of it. Belting the daylights out of unruly kids and a half dozen obnoxious drunks would provide an evening's entertainment and be perfectly good training for Rugby League Football, a pursuit that a number of them enjoyed. Saturday night provided good exercise for policemen; it was near enough the equivalent of your twenty-quid workout at the local gym these days – or maybe the last two years of your marriage, if you are both of an inclination to argue about everything. Unless you were courting or skint, Saturday nights in town were much of a much-ness, except at Christmas when alcohol-induced blurring later on in the evening came courtesy of *Technicolor*. While all that roistering was going on at our level, there would be other forms of entertainment in the town that we weren't privy to, such as the Press Ball and civic or private local-industry functions attended by the dinner suit and long gown people, plus The Coliseum would probably be offering productions for those of a more genteel nature. It's likely that the town catered for all tastes in entertainment, although we were never going to be exposed to most of it.

Goodness gracious, perish the thought!

11

The word "character" is used as a means of distinguishing people who are unlike the rest of us. I recall a couple of them from my wanderings about the town during the daylight hours. One of these was a man without legs who parked his means of mobility, which was a small "truck", next to the swing doors at the Curzon Street entrance to the Market Hall. The vehicle had two fixed wheels, one at each side in the middle and two smaller wheels, one to the front and the other at the rear of the truck, both sliding on short axles for manoeuvrability. The truck had two trough-type channels mounted on top of its frame to hold each of his upper thighs when he was in the sitting position. His leg stumps – the legs were missing from just above the knee – were bound in some sort of thick leather; he wore an old jacket, flat cap and knotted white silk scarf around his neck. He propelled his bogey with the aid of two ten-inch-long wooden pegs, pushing himself along with them. At weekends come rain or shine he was at his station outside the Market Hall doors at the top of Curzon Street. People gave him small-denomination coins as they passed him going into the Market Hall; he'd touch his cap-kneb in the time-honoured tradition as a gesture of thanks. When he got his wheels rolling he could really motor along. The bogey, at a guess, was two feet long and eighteen inches wide; the top of the carriage was approximately nine inches from the ground. The frame was fairly heavy and solid which made for a deep rumbling noise as the bogey progressed across the flags on Albion Street. People scattered in front of him like confetti in a hurricane. The man must have had great upper body strength. His method of getting home at around 6p.m. as the Market Hall was closing, was to wait on the pavement at the junction of Albion Street and Henshaw Street until a bus going his way came down Henshaw Street. He'd wave his arm at the driver who stopped his bus as near to the kerb as possible. The man got hold of the full-length handrail with one hand and flung his heavy bogey onto the bus platform hauling himself after it with the minimum of exertion. He stood on his stumps next to the compartment made for stowing prams and suitcases etc. under the stairwell of the bus. A wave of his hand to the driver and off they drove as if it was an everyday occurrence. I never knew where the man lived. He was redoubtable considering his predicament. Cut your finger today and it necessitates a visit to the hospital, three months' physiotherapy and a week off work – we don't know we're born do we?

Another character, I shall name him "Sam D.R. Other", was a Teddy Boy of some repute. That was immediately made known to us as we got off the bus on our first trip into town. Gossip had it that he and his brothers and their mates were a disruptive element in the otherwise smooth running of the town – I suppose there will have been instances of that happening. (It's gentle mockery; so previous administrators needn't be offended). Their unsociable habits meant dragging a few members of the local constabulary away from their more important pastimes – like whistling in the dark and having a pint in the Monkey Inn at the corner of Southgate Street and Waterloo Street. (Jesting again.) The gang's endeavours more than likely caused a lot of pencil sharpening, notebook seeking and an outbreak of reporter's-nose, within the walls of the *Oldham Evening Chronicle* buildings. As a result of their mischievous ways, the malcontents periodically generated a few column inches of space in the paper's nightly news edition. More seriously than that though, they pushed my father – seven years in the army during the Second World War – into commenting, 'Thi' need a bloody good hiding them buggers'.

At the time, he was speaking to Wilf our next-door neighbour. Wilf, whose house was across two dividing back garden walls – so the raising of voices was necessary – was in the Commandos during the same war and probably thought that they needed a bit more than that. I don't know how long the gang continued making a nuisance of itself in the town centre, nor did I ever stand in awe in their presence. Apparently they could be found at the Ritz skating rink on the corner of Lord Street and Rock Street on Saturdays. Teddy Boys were becoming obsolete in my day and those few that had survived until then were grouped together in the same category as Hell's Angels – a bit greasy and not overly fragrant.

Allied to the iniquitous pleasures of drinking were a number of dancehalls. Apart from the previously mentioned Savoy, we visited Hill Stores Ballroom, situated on the first floor of the Co-operative Building on Huddersfield Road at its junction with Ripponden Road, the Majestic Dancehall (or Ticker as it was known) in the vicinity of Cannon Street and Froggat's, somewhere in the area around Cross Street. The latter two were less well known to us – in fact I never entered either of them. At weekends, square dancing (dancing for "squares", foxtrot, waltz, etc.,) was the only dancing on offer at the Savoy and "Hill Stores". The Savoy Dancehall's owner, Tommy Smith, had his own dance-band and resident singers. Hill Stores Ballroom had a similar arrangement with dance bands, although that changed early on in my career as a weekend wastrel. Older clientele used the dancehalls on Saturday nights, greatly reducing the likelihood for bother – the type of bother that accompanies drunken, argumentative lads whenever females are around. Besides, if the Savoy bouncers wanted a workout there were two Rock 'n' Roll nights during the week when they could hone their brawling skills. I've been slung out of both premises, once by accident and once from necessity. I reckon that dances were held on the upper level of buildings so that people could admire and appreciate your free-fall technique as you bounced untidily down the stairs on your way to being ejected from the premises.

12

From the bus stop near The Butter Store on Henshaw Street you could hear Rock and Roll music from the Savoy loud and clear because the staff opened all the dancehall's windows to let some air into the place. Thinking about it now, the music was so loud, it could probably be heard at Rhodes Bank half a mile away. The whole of the teenage, fast-moving, a bit on the wild side ethos held a powerful attraction for me, I couldn't get enough of it. Backing music to most songs was fast and slightly orchestral, *Way Down Yonder In New Orleans* by Freddie Cannon and *Wild One* by Bobby Rydell to name a couple. Filling the swiftly flowing days and blurring one into the next, music was a strong undercurrent coursing through all of us. You'd hear teenagers trying to imitate Del Shannon when he was reaching for a high note, practically impossible without someone jabbing the singer with something sharp and shiny from mother's sewing basket. Life at the time was like a kaleidoscope, every morning we twisted the tube and out popped something new with a tune to match. I had the feeling of being alive, a part of something all-encompassing. I suppose the same thing happens to most youngsters with regard to the music of their time.

Ricky Nelson was a big name in the jukeboxes with *Hello Mary Lou*, *Never Be Anyone Else* and *Travellin' Man*.

> *Hello Mary Lou, goodbye heart*
> *Sweet Mary Lou I'm so in love with you*
> *I knew Mary Lou, we'd never part*
> *So, Hello Mary Lou, goodbye heart.*

Del Shannon shouted for his love quite forcefully, with his song *Runaway*. If his lady had been in the vicinity of Ringway Airport, she couldn't have helped but hear him.

Wishin' you were here by me
To end this miseree
An ah wonder, ah why why why why wonder
Why,
Why why why why why she ran away
An ah wonder, where she will stay-yay
My little runaway, a-run-run-run-run-runaway.

The Savoy was a wonderful place on nights during the week, given over to teenagers for three and a half hours or so per session. The dance floor was upstairs and had a small stage at one end – enough to fit a small dance-band and easily fitted the odd Rock 'n' Roll group hired for our entertainment. The overhead lighting was soft yellow in colour and wall-length mirrors at the far end of the room created the illusion of a much bigger place when it was full of kids. The dance floor was made from wood and particularly hard wood at that, you could hear the floorboards creaking like old wooden ships at anchor, as soon as you entered the building downstairs. Some records inspired the need for everyone up dancing, to stamp at certain parts of the song. After prolonged bouts of stamping the man responsible for the record player, Tommy Smith's brother, fearful of the downstairs ceiling's collapse, would stop the record with an ear-splitting screech as he lifted the armature from the record. He went on at great length to all enthusiastic stampers, advising them on the folly of their collective ways – meaning he wouldn't play that particular record again. After a lengthy amount of 'Aaawing' by the girls he returned the needle to the record and everyone carried on stamping. The walls were fitted with small soft-glow lamps and two yards or so of carpet ran around the edge of the dance floor, upon which stood a number of tables and chairs. When the upstairs curtains were closed, which they always seemed to be, even in mid-summer, the place had a warm shut-everything-out feel about it. The record player used was a portable one, situated next to the stage just around the corner from the top of the front stairs – the ones behind the entrance kiosk. A girl in our age group assisted Mr Smith with choosing and playing the records; I suppose she was conversant with the music trends of the time. I think that was her function. She was quite pretty.

Popular songs of the time were *Tallahassee Lassie*; *Poetry in Motion*; *You're Sixteen; You're Beautiful and You're Mine; Travellin'*

Man; *Cincinnati Fireball*; *Way Down Yonder in New Orleans*; *Sweet Nothin's*; *Dreamin'*; *Little Darlin'*; *Poison Ivy*; *Chain Gang*; *Will You Still Love Me Tomorrow?* *Since I Don't Have You*; *To Know Him is to Love Him*; *Runaway*; *Don't Tell Me Your Troubles*; *All I Could Do Was Cry.* I can't remember the names of all the singers, although if you were up for a bit of a crying, then Roy Orbison was your man. *Only the Lonely*; *Runnin' Scared* and later *Cryin'* were – probably still are – your best bet (Sigh). We'd have spent a lot of our time collectively crying if our song merchants had anything to do with it. No such thing as a dry summer in those years.

Curiously, American teenage singers were more popular with us than our homegrown products like Cliff Richard, Joe Brown, Adam Faith or Billy Fury; although *Oh Boy*, the Saturday night, early evening, television show had a good following. While rooting out the last whisker (well, bit of fuzz) from my freshly scrubbed, cherubic, little face, I'd be singing along with say Marty Wilde *Sea of Love* and the house would go quiet. Whether that was due to the beauty of my unique singing voice or just plain astonishment at the terrible noise coming from our bathroom, which had the same acoustic qualities as the inside of a biscuit tin, was difficult to determine. Most songs were made popular by television shows such as *Oh Boy* and *Juke Box Jury* and that great late-night friend of the lovelorn, Radio Luxembourg. American songs appeared in our music charts by the truckload, the Juke Box Jury panel panned many of those songs, yet when we went into town we couldn't get away from them. We had "experts" even in those days.

During the week the only dancing in teen-town was jiving at the Savoy. A lad nicknamed Robbo and his girlfriend were doing dance floor routines similar to John Travolta's, when Travolta was still wearing nappies. Everybody stopped dancing and formed a large circle in the middle of the floor while Robbo and his girl did their thing. Non-dancers spent their time observing the action whilst leaning against the walls; in doing the latter they probably stopped the walls from falling inwards due to the seismic shocks accompanying the loud music. Those wall-supporters who didn't seem to smile much were usually members of the tougheratti. While I didn't claim to belong to the latter, I was a fervent member of the former. I was born with two left feet, toe cruncher's syndrome or whatever your name for dysfunctional legwork might be. Long John Silver and I had much in common when it comes to rhythm and balance. There were a number of clever sods that could jive with two girls at the same time;

some of them must have had degrees in handbag hopping. (The practice of girls dancing around their handbags on the dance floor was a necessary one because of bag dipping by light-fingered folk. Stealing from handbags was made easy by the constant gloom surrounding the dance floor, a requirement to make dancing more attractive for the eager-but-shy or the spotty). The less clever of the two-girl dance men, took the occasional dive when the handbags weren't where they thought they should be on the dance floor – woefully embarrassing for him and extremely amusing for us with nods of admiration passing between the smirking observers. Be that as it may, those smart operators took two females out of the game at one go; further reducing the chances of lifelong happiness as a prospective mate for one of them. The fashion of the time was for unattached girls to dance in pairs (friends usually). One girl might be pretty, the other one less so. If you got two good-looking girls dancing together they were unlikely to be easily split up – that's just a comment not a fact. I suppose that the one who was left out would think, why did he ask her and not me?

There were two methods of entry into the Savoy on dark nights during winter, one through the doorway, having paid for the privilege, the other through the men's toilet window downstairs, which of course was free. Extra brownie points could be earned, should a lad be inclined to chance summary ejection himself, when caught admitting his pals by this method. At school I was reasonable at mathematics but I have never been able to work out the process of multiplication required to turn three lads walking into the toilets into ten lads walking out of them. The degree of difficulty was made even greater when this innocent-looking body of nonchalance had to pass directly in front of the eagle-eyed, management-related lady serving on the drinks counter. The chap taking money on the door sometimes took a pecuniary interest in the phenomenon when there was a lull in the arrival of customers. No matter how tightly the denim-clad micro-crowd grouped together, walked backwards or breathed in, the body mass stays the same. They might have been better off scattering like drops of water on a hot plate as they came through the toilet door. That way at least they might have had a drunk on a ladder's chance of staying inside the place. For those caught in the act, the sight of a rapidly approaching bouncer meant a walk straight out through the entrance door or a demand for the appropriate fee. A firm denial of illegal entry meant a quick march to the entrance kiosk with the bouncer dragging the bouncee along behind him. Upon arrival at the kiosk a formal request was made to the cashier to identify the individual as a paid-up person. If – in the time-honoured Roman tradition – the answer was a thumbs-down, the rapid propulsion of ones body through the exit door was to be expected. That depended upon how big you were of course. Sometimes removal required two bouncers – to my knowledge the men in red jackets never shirked their duty regardless of how many of them were needed in that task. The area where these fractious discussions took place was a step-up level from the ground floor and host to groups of tables and chairs all within easy reach of the soft drinks counter where you could also buy biscuits and crisps – stuff like that.

There were times on those mid-week nights when apathy was wandering around the building and no young man could summon up enough irritation to offer cranial reconstruction to another. There were similar nights, when even under the influence of Wilson's Mild beer, nobody felt the need to punch one of the three red-jacketed, sixteen-stone men standing around reading poetry or knitting. Tedium was a mentor that wasn't allowed much time to spread its weary message on most occasions though and a carelessly (or carefully) placed foot eventually tripped up a responsive lad thereby causing a major outbreak of hostilities to occur. When the participants in the scuffle were eventually parted, they left the premises a lot quicker than they'd entered. By accident or design, I'm not sure which, the large, double, fire exit doors were placed at the bottom of the far-end, dog-legged staircase. The bouncers had it made. One heave from the top step and without damaging any stairs on the way down, the ejectee, probably taking his first flight, was deposited on the first landing (so to speak). A similar exertion from there by the bouncers and the lad was poised on the brink of stardom. A quick crash on the fire doors' exit bar and the chap found himself contemplating the unevenness of the Council's paving arrangements along Cheapside – if he could still see that is. A final chastising clout to the head usually served as a memento of the occasion if the debate had been a fierce one. Finally the fire doors were slammed shut with a great show of enthusiasm and an over-the-top exhibition of hand dusting – the ejected ones could look forward to at least two weeks in the wilderness.

I starred in one of those little cameos once. Hostilities were satisfactorily under way as I arrived back inside the Savoy in mid-evening. A heaving mass of furious combatants tumbled down the stairs behind the dancehall's entrance kiosk, propelled by three eager bouncers. The paint-blistering language and ancestry-defining had nothing to do with me – I was just ambling round the corner of the kiosk on my way upstairs. The twenty-second cameo was very much like the comic strip cartoons that show a cloud with stars and other symbols; the odd red-sleeved arm would pop out and then a leg or a head accompanied by the brawlers' favourite word, which is 'Oooof'. Reflecting on the scene, it was free entertainment until one of the red sleeves lurched upright with a body attached to it and clocked me one in the face. A busted nose found its way onto my face as a consequence of this unforeseeable act. Ah! Receiving a haymaker is a very good way of losing interest in your surroundings for a while and plays hell with your deportment. It was a case of me being in the wrong place at the wrong time on the wrong night near the wrong stairs. I had been happily returning from the Odd House pub on Henshaw Street where I'd spent time reducing my intelligence levels by consuming a couple of pints of beer, when the incident occurred. The purpose of my return was to meet Jackie my girlfriend of the time, a stunningly beautiful, red-haired girl whom I adored. She had pale blue eyes and skin like porcelain, a figure to make the angels happy and could smile her way into the hardest heart. Ah, it was wonderful, this beautiful girl linking me as we went out – and I hadn't done anything to earn her, except clean my teeth and comb my hair. I lived so far away from town that I only got the smile three nights a week; but it was like the sun breaking through clouds. She could have walked into my heart, disconnected the pump and I would have lived for a further six months on the pleasure in knowing her – *you'll have gathered by now that I liked her.*

At the start of the night, most lads went to see 'Who was in' before they went on to the pub for an hour. I'd been polishing my introduction technique, consisting of hooking my thumbs into my belt loops, chewing spearmint gum slowly and staring at girls I fancied until they noticed me. Subtle stuff, hey?

You may well laugh; most lads' opening lines began with 'What ya doin' tonight darlin'?'

The girls usually riposted, quite loudly, with 'Get lost'. It was a favoured phrase of television sitcoms of the time and the first question of Bedouin desert dwellers or Arctic penguins when you turned up after wandering around the wastelands for a week without a compass.

I began to notice Jackie dancing with her friend at the mirrors-end of the dance floor. Girls generally jived on the same piece of turf each week. Some weeks after giving Jackie a regulation stare or two, her friend came and asked would I take Jackie home. I thought I would and said so. I remember it as if it were yesterday. Alarm bells should have been going off all over the place because I knew she was going out with someone else at weekends, I'd seen her at the pictures – but the bells stayed mute.

'Yeah, I'll meet her at the bottom of the steps at quarter to eleven,' I said, not wanting to appear too eager. That was it – I was in. The chat-'em-up lads didn't know a good technique when they saw one. My mind did five laps of the town shouting 'Eureka'. Meanwhile I walked my world staying cool as if it was my due after the long periods of staring that I'd recently put in. We both turned up at the pre-arranged time after the playing of the Savoy's traditional go-home anthem, *Save The Last Dance For Me* by The Drifters. I looked around for someone who might want to object to our meeting but no one made himself known. It wouldn't have mattered if anyone had offered an opinion, or wanted a fight, I was decidedly pleased with myself and wasn't in a giving-back frame of mind. Jackie worked on Hyde's Newspaper and Stationery stall in the Market Hall and she lived close to the dancehall, so walking her home wasn't a three mile hike. As has previously been noted, nothing more was expected of a decent girl than a nice turn out, a bit of adoration on their part and some rub-your-mouth-off kissing. That's how it was. In any case, to know what nothing was, a lad had to know what "something" was. Schools had no Human Methods Of Reproduction posters on the classroom wall when I was a six year old, I can tell you.

Returning to the uninvited assault on my nose by the bouncer, it didn't seem to take much to upset "the goons" in those days. The bouncer responsible probably didn't like my face and set about rearranging it, or maybe he fancied my girlfriend. Whatever, it cost me two hours in the Royal Infirmary on Union Street West, one week avoiding people as if I had the plague (some of which was spent with cotton buds jammed up my nose) and a large piece of sticking plaster to stop my nose from falling off. The lovely lady was deeply moved by my perceived lack of judgement. First for not informing her of my incapacity at the time and second that I was unavailable to take her home. I think there was a waiting period in which she had to establish whether she would be going out with a face that she was familiar with or moving on to pastures new. Once my nose had stopped pulsating like a lighthouse beacon and returned to something like its original shape, it passed Jackie's version of quality control and we carried on going-out for a while. In the end I had to go away for a few weeks with both of us swearing eternal devotion. Upon my return, the lovely girl was eternally devoted to someone else. When you're young, there's a current song to fit most occasions and The Shirelles got it just about right with the song that they're most famous for, *Will You Still Love Me Tomorrow?*

It was probably, the best "supplication" song of its time.

> *Tonight you're mine completely,*
> *You give your love so sweetly,*
> *Tonight the light*
> *of love is in your eyes,*
> *But will you love me tomorrow?*

Jackie's answer to that particular question was an emphatic 'No'.

A couple of months later I was asked if I wanted a re-match with her – Jackie's friend turned up on our doorstep at home with the request. You'll never know how strong the temptation was to say that I would. But, you know how it is with writing and walls.

Hah, well. *C'est la vie.* It does make me wonder where the hell we all thought we were going though, when first we set foot on the trail of love-tokens, transience and tears.

1. The policeman on point duty at the corner of Brook Street, under Mumps Bridge, Oldham, that David's father liked playing skittles with. *(Courtesy Oldham Evening Chronicle).*

2. The view from the other side of the bridge. Workman can be seen installing the new traffic light system to replace the policeman. *(Courtesy Oldham Evening Chronicle).*

3. Phil Cohen's shop on the corner near the old Victoria Market, Oldham, where David wiled away his time during daylight hours. *(Courtesy Oldham Local Studies and Archives).*

4. The Salisbury Hotel, near Mumps Bridge, was the starting off point on the circuit used by eager swains. It was demolished some years ago to make way for the small bus terminus near the present B & Q car park. *(Courtesy Oldham Local Studies and Archives).*

5. The old Savoy dance hall, which survived the demolition of much old property at the top of town, Oldham. *(Courtesy Oldham Local Studies and Archives)*.

6. The Savoy, which was a magnet for the young men attracted by young ladies and the beat of rock and roll. *(Courtesy Grumpy Photos Inc.)*.

7. Teenage girls jiving while waiting for their Prince Charming to emerge from the pub after drinking a few pints of 'Dutch Courage'. *(Courtesy Oldham Evening Chronicle).*

8. This is Bob, Lawrie, Terry and Jack – ready for anything. *(Courtesy Bob Marsden).*

9. Himself, posing in front of his dad's Ford Consul and pretending it's his – just in case a dolly was walking past.

10. Here's me hair – the rest is following! Is our man giving the photographer the hard look or is he fed up 'cos his sister, Jean, is tagging along? *(Courtesy Grumpy Photos Inc.).*

11. This is the preferred version of the last photo – without the sisterly encumbrance.

12. My mate Lawrie with the Elvis looks.

13. Lawrie with his beloved wife Kath, baby Julie and sister Pat in Australia.

13

Not long after that sobering episode, I was losing small amounts of sleep over a very good-looking girl in a fitted, cap-sleeved, little black dress, who appeared at the Savoy – fickle or what? (Those little black numbers have been causing havoc since we stepped from behind the fig leaf, discarded animal skins and sackcloth). The mode of dress was unusual because most girls wore flared skirts. She wore little make-up or jewellery and had dark straight hair worn at shoulder length. She never looked or smiled at anyone, not while I was assessing my chances at any rate. Enigmatic is the look that she was hoping to achieve, I suppose. She didn't know that she was responsible for my wakefulness and I thought that it would have made little difference if she had. Her friend was blonde-haired and equally striking, but she wasn't sparing with the application of face improver. The dark-haired young lady, on the few occasions that she turned up to grace the dance floor, had all of my requirements in a girl – all of them. I knew this was so without giving it any real thought, because I had refused to go for a drink with the rest of the lads in case I deprived her of the odd stare or two. All my interest-genes were fighting to get to the front of the pool. I hadn't any skin blemishes and made sure that there wasn't a hair on my head out of place. No dirty fingernails or buttons unfastened that shouldn't have been and I worked my razor blades into exhaustion, in my attempts to loom large in her sights. She couldn't have missed seeing me if she'd tried, she just didn't know how to interpret my tried and proven technique of staring and probably thought I was being rude. By now I'd improved that technique with the addition of a quick smile if the receiver looked my way – lads didn't smile much in those days. After a couple of weeks of being totally ignored, I cornered the blonde-haired girl downstairs at the drinks counter when she was alone and asked if her mate was available.

'She knows you're interested but won't go out with you', she said. With that she walked off back up the far end staircase to the dance floor.

Ho, ho, ho, my ego, which thought its rightful place was in the body of a famous person, jumped from my shoulder and went to sit on a windowsill until it could find a way to stop laughing.

In the next stampede for the pub I decided that it was my duty to "down a few", which usually brought forth the Genie Who Solves Problems – more particularly mine of the time. Having paid the next instalment on the mortgage of The Odd House pub's landlord, we were on our way back into the dancehall when the dark-haired girl stopped me just inside the front door, which threw me a bit. It was very noisy, even downstairs in the dancehall, so she suggested that we go outside. A nod to the cashier earned us each a pass-out (a small white card with the date stamped on it) so that we could return later, without paying again.

By this time the recently-consumed beer was running around inside me as if the devil was chasing it with a shovel full of hot coals; at the same time I thought it was Christmas Day, Cup Final day, my birthday and payday, all rolled into one. After I'd mumbled something banal to her, she said that she was sorry but she already had a boyfriend who was in the army but she was going to pack him in when he came home on leave. Not on my account, she'd added smiling; but even at that age reasoning suggested that I was in with a shout or she wouldn't have told me. How pathetic can you get? All I could do was babble inanities while we leaned against a window ledge across from the front door of the dancehall. I hadn't rehearsed what I would say if a meeting ever came about, because I hadn't really expected one and nervousness wasn't one of my usual conditions I assure you. I'm not usually reticent in running off at the mouth either. After ten minutes of her talking and me listening, we walked back into the dancehall. I got the smile again before she went back upstairs and that was me, well and truly snookered. You can't find yourself in No Man's Land by the very nature of the saying, but I sure as Hell didn't know exactly where I was. Still, you had to see the girl to know that she was exquisite. I cut back on the pints of mind-loosener and kept myself as cool as a lollipop on an iceberg over the next week. I was living in hope – well I lived in Moorside, but hope was the next stop after that and thereby hangs the tale. You paint your own pictures in life and I couldn't paint to keep the world spinning. Believe me, we would all have fallen off the planet long ago, if its turning had depended upon my dreams turning into actuality. I had a nagging feeling in the depths of my mind on the way to the Savoy the following Monday, that the pub would soon be crooking its finger at me again.

And so it was. I never saw the girl or her friend again, didn't even know her name. She may have changed her mind about her boyfriend; it certainly wasn't me at fault if she did. I could show reasonable references; I dressed for the times, was acne-free and sweat wasn't allowed in our house. Nay, I had a bath once a week – or was it twice a month? Hmm, there was a well-beaten trail leading to our bathroom, with little white arrows sign-posted at strategic points along the way. If a bar of soap didn't need replacing within the week, then I'd better come up with a damn good reason why not – our mother was keen on clean.

The girl had worn tiny earrings that flashed in the light strobes shining from two, many-faceted mirror-globes hanging from the dancehall ceiling, which turned lazily – when someone thought to switch them on. The beams occasionally caught her beautiful dark-brown eyes, which perfectly matched her hair; she looked like a ghost when the reflected light caught her on its unhurried way round the room. I could think that she was a ghost, these many years later. It's a peculiarity of the human condition that we store in memory the few people that we might have liked, along with the hundreds that we haven't liked of course.

Speaking of hair brings me to the subject of a peculiar hairstyle prominent amongst young ladies around that time and known as the bouffant or Beehive. The style was enough to make even the least inquisitive amongst us wonder what the heck the girls might be hiding under those spring-loaded creations. More to the point what were they thinking they looked like. Humidity inside the dancehalls was quite high and jiving is a frenetic pastime. During the evening quite a few girls developed the appearance of a dishevelled porcupine on its way home from a syrup spraying demonstration at Tate and Lyle. When I was being attentive rather than my usual gormless self, a close inspection of the style revealed the amount of backcombing needed to bring this style to life and must have been time consuming. The distressing ants-nest appearance of the hair was often accompanied by the girl blowing large chewing gum bubbles which sometimes popped and stuck all over her nose and lower face. Some girls performed those back combing rituals in public, often while admiring their reflection in shop windows, or a friend would hold up a handbag mirror for her to look into. I saw one girl in Blackpool doing maintenance in the reflection of a pair of those mirror sunglasses popular at the time. Sometimes during those operations the girl did a bit of hip swinging accompanied by her mindlessly singing or humming the tune to a popular song. In tune-free girls the utterances came in a different key than the one intended by the songwriters and musicians and identifying the song was something of a challenge. I never had any intention of going out with a girl who wore her hair in a bouffant style – which narrowed my field of choice considerably. Nor had I much sympathy with the lads who accompanied these mini-monuments when they were subjected to the rigours of a good north-easterly wind. Being fashionable is one thing, courting disaster is quite another. Imagine yourself as a young lad, walking down the street arm in arm with a girl, rigged out in her best battle-dress and a backcombed, fine-mesh, lacquer-plastered, hair-do that closely resembled a bishop's mitre. If the wind decided to rock it, what would you do? Run round and round the girl with your hands held out, hoping to catch the blessed thing if it snapped off. There was rain of course, which took great delight in reducing the style into something more at home in a tree with eggs in it. There was also the thorny question of what to do with the hairy construction when engaged in back-row exertions at the cinema. I have seen girls wobbling onto the paved area at the front of the Gaumont cinema with sloping bouffant very much like the ones that the Pharaoh kings heaped daub and affection upon. If the movie was a horror film then that would go some way towards explaining why the hair was lying at such an acute angle to the top of their heads. To complement this type of hair-do, many girls wore puff shouldered blouses, tight skirts with Waspie belts (three-inch wide, black elasticated belts with a clasp at the front) three-inch stiletto heels, which left the girl in between hair and shoes looking like the filling in a Picasso-inspired sandwich. In my youth, discounting the Beehive, girls looked and carried themselves considerably better than some of the female creations that come tumbling out of pubs and clubs these days, shouting profanity and vomiting all over the place.

I have a friend from my youth, who later became a workmate for many years. Dave's fairly relaxed and doesn't give too much of a monkeys about most things. He told me one day when we were rehashing old times, that he had a sure-fire way of not being seen out sober with a girl who was less desirable than others of the sisterhood. Dave liked a drink; one of the inevitable consequences of that liking was a lowering of his sights in the pursuit of females. (Everything, excluding optimism, gets lowered after a three-hour bout with brain cleaner). Usually, it was a girl he'd met at Hill Stores dancehall on Saturday night. He had a system for making future arrangements when any girl asked him if he would be seeing her again. He'd arrange to meet her outside one of the cinemas in town and on the chosen night and time ride past the cinema on the No.59 bus. The bus stopped outside most of the cinemas on its route. If the girl didn't match up to his expectations when he spotted her – if he could remember her at all – he would stay on the bus and go from there for a couple of pints; there were always some mates around town who didn't have a date themselves. He didn't say what he did if there were a lot of girls waiting for their respective dates and he couldn't recognise the appointed one, maybe it was a matter of elimination-by-waiting. Given that option it would be a simple matter to stand around the nearest corner and see who was left over.

There's a wait-a-minute gene in young lads with regard to female selection and it appears when a plain girl hauls up on the horizon. You take them on for a variety of reasons, some of which are of a discreet nature, but mostly just to fill in your time. I'm sure that girls are party to exactly the same type of reasoning. Other than your genes having some subliminal contact with the genes of the prospect-less one, I can't think how it works. It could be a personality thing I suppose. In my time I've heard a couple of reasons why the "wait-a-bit" thing occurs; one from an educated chap named Gerald who said 'They're girls less representative of their gender and you wouldn't be improving the species if they produced offspring.'

The other chap, known as M.T. (empty) owed his philosophical insights to the venerable school of alcoholic appreciation. He would proclaim from deep within his fume-filled hole, in a voice that all and sundry could hear, often in reference to someone's intended, 'If you 'ave any girls by 'er, they aren't likely to win the Miss Universe Contest are they? Face like a jug full of oysters, she'as." M.T. was often reprimanded for his contentious views – sometimes with briskly-applied force. Men were a little chauvinistic in those days.

Maybe more than a little – I suppose it was a lot really.

Sometimes they overdosed on it altogether.

WHEN ELVIS SANG

Dress was full drape and link button and cutaway collar turned up.
Your belt had studs and horse buckle, which helped to develop the strut.
Shoes never meant to be walked in, crepe in blue indigo suede.
A large polished buckle in silver and white nylon socks made the grade.
Hairstyles were born at the movies, Dion, Rick Nelson and such.
The narrowest jeans on the market, with turn-ups and tight at the crutch.

Monday nights pulsated music, with dancing playing its part.
Elvis the man for all reasons sang softly over your heart.
The Trap Inn owned the best jukebox, The Oddhouse served underage beer.
Dark The Savoy, yet beguiling, romance often wandered in here.
Tommy Smith, round and good-natured, was master of all he surveyed.
Except for the toilet room window, where hard-up young lads hadn't paid.

Renting your heart but unsmiling, she lived in a chewing gum smile.
Like most of the girls in your world she whirled, for many a musical mile.
An unguarded smile might be given, whenever your cool eyes roamed.
The welcoming drink of acquaintance cost the price of your bus fare home.
Ah, love could be in an interested glance, returned by a stare on your part.
Hit-parade love was unending, for all knew the words off by heart.

Bouncers, nice blokes in red jackets, stood watching the talent sway by.
Fair in the least altercation – everyone got a black eye.
Non-jiving blokes got up dancing, their reticence somewhat allayed,
Towards the end of the evening, as the smoochiest records were played.
I suppose that my vision's rose tinted, but then who the hell gives a hang.
The world was a beautiful, wonderful place, on the nights that Elvis sang.

David J. Lavisher   July 1995.

14

An illustration of the violence in the town and its tendency to pop up when least expected, occurred one night as I was walking to catch the last bus home after taking Jackie home from the pictures. Approaching the bus stop opposite the Snipe Inn on Henshaw Street, I found two lads leaning on the elbow-rail in what I thought was deep, friendly conversation.

'How do', I said to one of them, who was a couple of years older than me and lived in our village of Moorside. I stepped away from the bus stop, not wanting to be thought an eavesdropper. The other lad I'd seen knocking around town occasionally – knocking being an appropriate word – with his girl friend. Without any notice of intent, there was a short flurry of blows and the lad from our village was soon lying on his back contemplating the stars in the sky – as well as the ones that came with the exchange of blows of course. When I had eventually pulled the unknown chap off him, at some risk to my personal safety, he roared something unintelligible to the figure recumbent on the pavement before walking off up Henshaw Street, collecting his girl – whom I hadn't seen – from the deeply recessed doorway of the fabrics shop near the bus stop. Our man was left holding his head, which was beginning to look like a piece of raw beef. The bus came and we boarded it, along with a few mates who had arrived by this time. I asked him what the debate was all about. Holding his face together with *my* handkerchief, he said that he and some mates had been in The Odd House pub most of the night and although the couple were in the room they were in, he'd not taken much notice of them. All the same, the girl didn't think that the latter bit was the case and complained to her chap about it. She'd said that our man kept staring at her and she felt uncomfortable – bear in mind that the room was only big enough to whittle a stick in, so he was bound to look in their direction occasionally. It seemed as if our lad had broken the eleventh commandment, "Thou shalt sit there all night with thine eyes averted, in the presence of petulant women".

At that age and speaking of commandments, I couldn't see what all the fuss was about really, the girl had obviously never heard of the twelfth commandment, "Thou shalt not weigh more than thy refrigerator"; she was, to put it politely, a big-un.

What men will do for love, eh! Love propped up by a couple of quarts of Wilson's beer and a girl who liked to see blood on the paving flags.

15

One member of our happy band of delinquents, Terry, worked for a plastic raincoat making company named Pakamac. The firm had taken over a section of the defunct Moorside Mill on Northgate Lane in our village. (I tell you, I couldn't have wished for a better bunch of mates if I'd asked a genie to supply them). Terry was a motivator and instigator of all things youthful and interesting. The lad was top drawer, had a great sense of humour and was up for practically anything. He dressed in the very best clobber and was a girl-catcher – but better than all of those other attributes, he didn't borrow money from you. The company that he worked for was very generous with its employees from a recreational point of view. They provided two football teams in the Oldham Amateur League, subsidising them with complete kit including boots and provided transport to away matches with its own mini-bus from the factory. The first team, Pakamac Panthers, was a very good team and won most of the trophies on offer in its time. Football was organised by the son of the company's owner, (who wasn't as mentally balanced as he should have been). He was expansive, excitable and spent money as if he was dealing playing cards. It was said that he had a brilliant mind as a young man, with a university education and then he suffered some kind of breakdown. Whatever we required in the way of football accoutrements he bought without question – a bit like the way Manchester United Football Club treats its pampered players these days I suppose. Improving upon that example of their generosity though, the company provided an annual works dance at Belle Vue, Manchester. Either the company had a relaxed attitude to workers bringing along a few friends or we were allowed to go because we played for the soccer team. I'm not sure but I suspect the latter.

Dance night turned up, it was Friday, and we made our own way to the Cumberland Suite at Belle Vue, missing the coaches provided for the purpose through fooling around. Once inside the Belle Vue grounds we passed a few exhibits of the usual fairground kind and came upon a booth displaying a real woman's head atop a painted snake's body on a mural on the back wall of the booth. The snake's body ran up the wall say eight feet from the floor of the stage with the lady's head protruding through a neck-sized hole. Her body was hidden somewhere behind the façade but we couldn't determine the means of the deception. The woman was exceptionally good-looking and world class at keeping still, not batting an eye-lid as we walked around the booth trying to work out how the illusion was created. Nobody had a decent brain cell to apply to the problem – we were going to a dance and they weren't required – so the brain cells that were on duty decided to improvise and came up with the idea of someone throwing a small pebble at the lady's head, which still hadn't moved.

The stone was cast.

The head hardly moved as it said with wonderful diction and clarity, 'Now, #^?* %//.'

So we did, with some alacrity.

Someone shouted to her, as we left, 'No need to get excited, it wasn't a half 'jocker''

A 'jocker' was a red building brick – I don't know why it was so named.

Reflecting on the occasion, nobody seemed disturbed at the crisp epithet that had issued from such fair lips as hers.

The dance was in half-swing when we walked through the suite's large glass doors and made headway towards the bar. Once our fuel tanks were in receipt of their first few swallows of beer, it was customary for us to take two steps back from the bar and do a quick appraisal of the available girls on display and then do a further sweep of the ones spoken-for (even at that age we'd worked out that attached girls sometimes detached themselves for a short while later on in the evening). Noting the "possibles", we sat at a table to ease-up on our social restrictions and to clown around a bit.

Girls seemed to dance in pairs until about 9.00p.m. No lad worth his salt thought to ask any girl to dance so early in the evening, I don't really know why, maybe it was to keep the business of buying them drinks to a minimum. There is a mechanism to "enable" non-dancers at these functions. It's a simple one. At 8.00 p.m. can't dance – drink plenty of beer. At 9.30 p.m., still can't dance – but think you can. If you're not a natural hoofer, the easiest way to learn to dance is through a fair intake of fermented hops, never mind all that dancing school stuff. A pint or two usually permits you to produce dance steps that the dancing schools have never heard of. At around the 9.30pm high tide mark, older ladies like to get you on the dance floor and whirl you around a bit, your lack of inhibition being pretty obvious from the many empty beer glasses stacked on your table. The ladies are unconcerned about possible broken toes, where your hands let if you are going to fall over, or whether you are doing the correct dance steps. I've also noticed that through it all they smile – they smile a lot. Once those good ladies have bolstered your confidence you look around for someone who *does* mind having her feet stepped on and where you position your hands.

On this occasion Terry indicated across the room with a nod of his head towards two pretty blonde girls, both wearing the same type of salmon pink coloured dresses. He'd been keeping an eye on them and they were unattached as far as he could see. Turning towards me he pointed at them with his forefinger, which was a bit bent at the end, exposing three inches of white shirt-cuff and highlighting his red, Roman gladiator's head cuff links.

'Seize 'em', he said imperiously and we ambled over slowly, to let them view the goods coming their way. The girls were agreeable to our polite requests and we shuffled onto the dance floor. Where older ladies hold you tightly, young ladies keep the obligatory nine inches away from you until they get to know you better, making it difficult to step on their toes or interfere with their hair or anything else for that matter. They were still with us at the end of that dance and able to walk, so we must have acquitted ourselves well.

Buying drinks for girls that I don't know was something that I didn't enjoy. Not that I'm tight fisted or anything, but I didn't like to waste what few resources I had in applying drink to girls, even though it was standard practice amongst men who usually had an ulterior motive. I broke the bank that time and treated the girl I was with to a vodka and lime. Ah, what the hell, she was pretty and Ray, the proprietor of our local chip shop, wasn't going to go bust if he didn't get the price of my Wednesday night bag of pie and chips the following week.

We danced our little white socks off for the rest of the night, neither Terry nor I losing sight of each other in the press of swaying bodies. While we were taking a men's-room break we agreed not to miss the coaches going back to town. Our pooled resources wouldn't let us look at a taxi, never mind ride in one. As luck would have it (or not) the girls lived at Werneth, somewhere off Oxford Street, Oldham, so we did the honourable thing and got off the coach to escort them home. Once the girls had paid the price for our protection – a bit of lip mashing – they agreed to a double date on the following night, which was Saturday. The walk from Werneth to Moorside is longer than long, not grumble-worthy though with a few pints of immunity still wandering around in your system, and it was quite safe in those days. We didn't turn up for the pre-arranged date due to lack of funds; Terry got it in the ear for five minutes from one of the girls at work on Monday morning and that was the end of that.

16

Some eight weeks before my seventeenth birthday, which falls on Spring Day in March, my mother decided that for a birthday present I should have a driving licence for cars. It was pretty far-sighted of her at the time; previously I hadn't driven anything bigger than a motorbike that my dad had cobbled together, a 350cc Ariel in fact. She thought that adding a car licence was in my best interests – which she always had at heart – regardless of the consequences for the Borough's pedestrians. Even though I didn't have a car and there was nothing winking from the horizon to suggest that I would have one in the near future, Mother managed to convince the British School of Motoring that I had most of my faculties intact and in exchange for £13 exactly, she asked them if they would provide me with a measure of driving ability suitable to impress a driving-test examiner. They agreed to her request, thereby removing safe passage upon The Queen's Highways during my lifetime. Winter, in the middle of January, is not a good time to be taking your first tenuous steps into four-wheeled motoring. In addition to that, there is a possibility that you will bankrupt a few insurance companies and disturb any number of slumbering policemen on your way to gaining driving competence. It's even worse when the only tuition possible was on nights during the week due to my work obligations. The commencement date arrived and clutching my provisional licence in my sticky little fist I presented myself at the driving school premises on Union Street, which was situated next door but a few to Harry Butterworth's chip shop. After a swift appraisal of my licence and a doubtful look in my direction, one of the driving instructors led me outside to view a reasonably new, unscratched, Triumph Herald motor car. He drove us both (me and the car) to Waterloo Street and gave me some rudimentary instructions on how pulling this does that and not to forget where the brakes were positioned because people don't like being knocked off their feet, especially if they're carrying beer or babies. Over a period of a few weeks at one hour, two nights per week, the instructor rubbed the edges off my natural aggressiveness and the three of us got along satisfactorily, except when we practised an emergency stop one time and he ended up under the dashboard in a jumble of profanity and sheets of paper. Cars didn't have seat-belts in those days and I had pretty sharp reflexes; it's through being scared a lot as a child. Nights when I rode past the driving school office on the bus, I could see through the front window that there were people sitting at desks in the large, well-lit, open-plan room. When I presented my happy little face through the door some minutes later, there might be a smouldering, half-smoked cigarette relaxing in an ashtray or a cup of coffee steaming on the desk, but no sign of human habitation whatsoever. Call me paranoid if you like, but that doesn't happen when you go into a cake shop or moneylenders. I'd take a seat (not actually take one) until someone summoned up enough courage to come out of hiding. The lessons cost a pound each with a pound for the licence and whatever the cost of the test-fee was, (the driving school applied for the test date). So, after a couple of near dos and a lot of rude comments from pedestrian members of the public, the instructor thought that I would probably achieve the desired pass upon taking the driving test. My series of lessons finished, the driving school left me to my own devices for two weeks, which is odd when you think about it, practice making perfect and all that.

At 9a.m,. two hours before my driving test was due, I turned up at the driving school to have a double driving lesson. That was unfamiliar territory. In daylight I could see further down the road than I had been able to do at night and I began to notice large lorries, absent from the roads at night and there were a lot more buses careering around the streets.

'Ha, Ha, Haa.' Far worse than that though, the Triumph Herald had been busy while I was away from it. It had entered a period of metamorphosis from which it emerged as a Ford Anglia. I don't recall the reason given for the missing Triumph Herald, maybe someone had crunched it, but I wasn't ecstatic about the change of vehicle – that I well remember. Anyone who has driven a Triumph Herald will tell you that they have a very tight turning circle, which would be why driving schools used them. The Ford Anglia had difficulty turning into a side street never mind anything else; it might have been better if it had turned itself into a tank. There was no form of heating present in the car – unless we had a near miss with a pedestrian or another vehicle, also it had a tendency to wander across to the other side of the road. Correcting the deviation meant turning the steering wheel perhaps a sixth of its circumference, before there was any discernible response. The knob on the end of the gear stick was positioned at about elbow height. Swaying about like an angry cobra it was difficult

106

to grasp in order to change gear, but eventually, aided by silent swearing, I was able to apprehend it. While we were patrolling the streets, there was often an unsatisfactory clunking sound as the next gear in sequence was engaged. The instructor thought I should let the clutch in quicker, so I did and for a while we kangaroo'd our way down the road like rodeo riders at the Calgary Stampede. Initially I didn't seem to have enough hands to change gear, operate switches and keep the damn thing in a straight line whilst trying to drive in the same direction as the rest of the traffic.

'You'll soon get used to it', the instructor said, as we zig-zagged down Union Street hoping we didn't attract the attention of policemen, one of whom was detailed every day to prop up the Star Inn in case it might fall down. At various points during the stint, whenever it thought I was being nasty with its clutch or gearbox, the car set off very determinedly for Manchester Street (presumably heading home to the Ford factory at Dagenham). With the introduction to the new car completed and the instructor having recovered some of his composure, we set off in earnest fashion to interfere with the smooth flow of traffic for what was left of the two hours. Eventually we got our act into something resembling cohesion and made steady progress along the roads. Two hours later, chock full of optimism and with the instructor wanting to chew my finger nails because he had none left of his own, we set off for the test circuit, which I knew off by heart by then.

As the instructor and I walked towards the test centre at number 72 Union Street, Oldham, I tried to memorize every number plate within what I considered to be the required twenty-odd yards from the test centre's front door. I was absolutely convinced that the examiner would ask me to read one of these as we stepped from the building to begin the driving test. (As a matter of interest, there was nothing wrong with my eyesight and he didn't ask me to read a number plate until we stopped at the top of Park Road at its junction with King Street some fifteen minutes later). The driving instructor let out a deep breath and said a rude word when the chap with the clipboard made himself known to us in the test centre. When I asked the instructor, out of the corner of my mouth, what was wrong, he whispered out of the corner of his mouth, 'You've got the chief examiner and he's a right *^/#-%î.'

You'll have guessed that I was absolutely brimming over with confidence at that news.

Not the type of confidence that inspires lippy-ness with twenty stone wrestlers or making the intimate acquaintance of a 500lb. lion without a .475 calibre rifle to hand – more the confidence of a man about to smile at a firing squad. In the event I ran the route, did the turns and reverses, kept to my own side of the road, admired myself in the interior mirror the recommended amount of times. We did the braking distances; sequences of traffic lights, what I should do if a chicken crossed the road, all those kinds of thing. I was so nervous and naïve I thought I had failed the test. The examiner wrote out a pink slip and handed it to me saying, 'Watch your wing mirrors more often'. Prior to him saying that, I'd thought that wing mirrors were fitted to make a car look pretty, they were too far away down the wings of the car to be of any other use. I suppose, upon reflection, that he may have said, 'Wash your wing mirrors more often.'

I fully expected a pass to be written on a foolscap-sized piece of white paper, which detailed your driving excellence, humane qualities and visual perceptiveness. Those were not precisely the words I was thinking, but you can see where I was heading. When the instructor came "yipping" down the pavement after the examiner had left the scene, I thought he'd cracked up.

'Bloody marvellous, I saw him hand you the pink slip,' he said, 'First time pass, I knew you'd do it'. Which wasn't the impression he'd left me with twenty-five minutes earlier. The public at large, multitudes of passengers and a few vehicle insurance companies have had ample reason to rue that day's work.

Ah well, a few excursions into a couple of girls' charms, nothing worth a mention here, except maybe the girl who lived on Ashton Road and drank more than Terry, Lawrie, Bob and me put together. She was a nice looking girl, but she was bouncing off the walls by 9.30p.m. She must have been born with an inflatable overflow tank hidden about her body somewhere. Considering the amount of liquid that she consumed at any given time she very rarely troubled the ladies facilities. It was my pockets that didn't like her – they just couldn't afford her. Shortly after that affair I put my nightlife, town-nurtured sophistry, lightly tarnished reputation and my comb, into a suitcase and headed for The Promised Land. Which for my purposes was Saddleworth.

17

Back in the mists of time, long before Oldham Metropolitan Borough Council got its sticky fingers on it, the Urban District of Saddleworth was a pleasant place to spend time; green and serene would best describe it. The area was liberal in both its politics and its generosity towards outsiders. Long periods of peace and quiet were the norm in the villages and those seemed to be broken only when gaps occurred in the softly hissing winds blowing off the moors. During the week, filling those gaps were loud, metal-clanking noises produced by operating machinery, heard perhaps when someone opened a door into the weaving shed of a nearby woollen mill. Occasionally, the desultory sound from jackhammers smashing tarmac on the district's road surfaces drifted up on the breeze when road menders were about their business. Wherever sunlight fell, it formed a golden tranquillity, basked in by those of us too long used to the loud, frenetic, rock and roll world over the south-west side of the hills. Saddleworth was an outpost of the West Riding of Yorkshire and its string of villages typical of the series of small stone-built ones to be found some six miles to the east of its boundaries in Huddersfield and beyond. The area was pretty well laid back, at ease with itself and the outside world; there was a casual acquaintanceship amongst its working people. Its industries – principally woollen mills – complemented each other and therefore people moved about between the different firms, becoming known to each other from as far apart as Denshaw and Greenfield. The people of the three valleys that make up the North and Eastern end of Saddleworth got on with their rural type of life in peace.

It would be some time in the future before its dwellings were so priced that you'd need to win the lottery, have connections with the Mossley Mafia or own a second-hand car dealership in order to buy into what is, supposedly, Saddleworth's exclusivity. These days if a person were to put curtains in a telephone box in Saddleworth, someone would pay a fortune to live in it. Today the valleys are home to city escapees, people who pronounce their aitches and are possessed of large mortgages and second homes. Within its boundaries live a selection of artists of one kind or another and of course there is the cachet of the celebrated writer/poet Ammon Wrigley having been a Saddleworth man. Now that the industries have gone, it's reasonable to suppose that public meeting places like pubs, churches, and various other groups with particular interests are the only common ground on which people meet regularly these days.

Apart from those who just wanted a quiet life, the major influx of people coming to live in the countryside started with the old barn and farmhouse renovators and progressed to television personalities, producers and other wannabe-somebody-somewheres, until it arrived at its present place. They were, by and large, people who hadn't lived in the countryside previously. If I haven't smiled for a while, I remember this little anecdote about one family's expectancies. Dragging their Bentley Continental from the garage, some newly-arrived individuals went straight round to the Council offices to complain about the terrible smell they had to put up with because the local farmer was spreading cow-muck in the fields beyond their garden wall. (I kid you not!).

Some of those early immigrants departed to milder climes when the height of snow in winter reached five or six, sometimes ten feet. Ah, bless 'em! Snow isn't good for Gucci shoes or Christian Dior clothing. A few of my companions of the time found it chuckle-worthy that some of those aspirants to countryside living would take a three-week winter holiday abroad. Upon arrival, they'd play bloody hell if there wasn't enough snow on the ground to ski.

Saddleworth is a good all-year-round place to live now that winter appears to have toned down its act a little. Good that is, apart from where the town's planners and some silken-voiced builders have and still are tinkering with it. Let sleeping dogs be up and about, seems to be their motto.

Saddleworth proper runs down the valleys from Denshaw through to Greenfield, incorporating the villages of Delph, Dobcross, Diggle and Uppermill en route. Someone might take issue with that statement because the outer reaches include Scouthead, Grasscroft, Springhead and Friezland. Be that as it may, the district was administered to and serviced by offices and depots within the villages.

In my youth, Saddleworth had its own area police force and the district's doings were attended to locally, perhaps partly funded and overseen by the West Riding Authority (based in Wakefield) for its greater financial affairs. Oldham Metropolitan Borough Council now administers Saddleworth in the collection of its dues and the processing of its needs, although the boundaries were never changed and Saddleworth still resides within the original Yorkshire county boundary – but on the Lancashire side of the Hill.

Some of its children with the need for higher education were sent out of the district to study at schools in Oldham and Huddersfield. A number of bus services ran through the area, the North Western Road Car Co., Oldham Corporation Transport, Hanson Buses and a service ran through the village of Denshaw towards Oldham from Ripponden and back again, a company whose name I cannot recall. There were sufficient shops throughout the area to cater for everyday needs, larger domestic items necessitating a trip to facilities with a wider range of choice at the aforementioned towns or the cities of Leeds and Manchester.

From an outsider's point of view, Saddleworth life was an oasis, a little pocket of rusticity spread over the five north eastern villages. The people had their own accent, which leaned heavily on its Yorkshire origins. The area was generally quiet other than on local celebratory days. I suppose you could say that they had their very own Eden. You wouldn't think so now of course. To my mind, Eden only exists as two thirds of Sweden. In those days many young people wanted to leave the area as soon as they were able, primarily because it lacked variety in commodity and entertainment. Now most young people can't stay even if they want to, the price of property being what it is. There has been no significant increase in permanent attractions other than the restoration of the Huddersfield Narrow Canal, although I did recently hear of a gripe for a superstore to be built in Greenfield. Once the boulder starts to roll ... . Not a nice thought!

18

It was early in the evening, around mid-November 1961, and very cold. Leaning back against the freestanding road-sign at the end of Friarmere Road in Delph village I looked across the valley towards Knott Hill where a crescent moon hung just above the horizon and seemed to be staring back at me in mockery at my recent predicament. The thin sliver of moon was surrounded by a wispy haze and resembled a semi-circular shard of opaque glass from the bottom of a shattered Lalique vase. I thought about moving into the empty telephone box because of the cold, but thought better of it – cold is cold, inside or outside. The hills surrounding the village were dark and had been quiet, now there was an eager thump-thump-thumping from the engine of a Velocette Viper motorbike, growling its way down Grains Road towards the village centre.

Grains Road, along with Denshaw Road and Millgate, is one of the main entrance roads to the village; there are three other minor roads that also service the village.

In the darkness the bike's headlight seemed to drop down the hillside like a large leaping white stone that had been thrown down a cliff face. I knew it was John Buckley – Buck as he was known in the village. When you're hanging around the same motorbikes regularly, you begin to recognise their individual exhaust-pipe sound. The fishtail exhaust pipe on the Velo' gave a unique and easily recognisable sound. Grains Road was John's personal stretch of racetrack and about two miles long. He opened the throttle on his motorbike at the King's Arms pub at Grains Bar and shut it off at the Bull's Head pub in the village.

The sound of records being played, a few decibels below the point at which the windows start to crack, in a house on Roche Road to the left and behind me, wasn't to my liking so I gathered what laughingly passed as my accoutrements, motorbike helmet, gloves, etc., and set off riding into the village to see if anyone was about. The Velocette and rider were coming towards me as I rode past the Eagle Garage at the beginning of Denshaw Road. Its rider raised his hand as he rode past, face hidden behind goggles and crash helmet; he looked wild, as if the Hounds of Hell were chasing him – or maybe the Devil. Perhaps both of them were after him, knowing the rider as well as I do. He always rode as if something was after him, that's for sure. When I arrived in the village it was empty, not even a door bang or the lingering whiff of cigarette smoke. I decided to go for a pint in the Swan Inn on the village's main street; bar the landlord, the place was like a ghost town. While I set about emptying a couple of glasses I thought of how I had set foot on the long and not unpleasant road leading to that present moment.

19

'Are you out of collar?' asked Wilf's elder son Tony, one Saturday night on his way out with his mates.

Wilf and his family lived next door to us in Moorside. Tony worked at the brickworks just over the hill. ('Collar' is a colloquialism for yoke or work).

'Nearly' I replied.

'They want some at ours; it's hard work but the money's good, shall I ask for you on Monday?'

'Yeah, if you will,' I replied.

I could do hard work – 'course I could. I cleaned my own shoes, never spilled any beer that I had bought myself and I got out of bed before eleven o'clock in the morning on Sundays. When I was young, all that went under the heading of hard work. My brain wasn't used to hard work however, it had been asked on numerous occasions but never seemed to get around to implementing it. For instance, I had thought – when I thought at all in those days – that *ad hoc* was the last minute addition of a bottle of wine to the bottom of a grocery list and that *Victor Ludorum* was a Danish/Jewish pianist. I've carried on serenely through my life with the latter in mind, until a few years ago, when I was informed amidst much merriment and loud barracking that it is Latin for overall winner or supreme victor. Somewhat embarrassing if you're as smart as I think I am.

Well, Victor Borge sounds a bit like *Victor Ludorum* – doesn't it?

Anyone reading this narrative who was in my class at school will not be surprised by that last revelation. I remember one year at secondary school, when a male teacher occasionally enjoyed an early morning row with his wife, after which he would enter the classroom with the sole intention of taking his ire out on the first pupil who got an answer wrong. He'd stride about in high dudgeon and I recall quoting him a load of old rubbish in reply to one of his questions. He told the whole class and perhaps half of the school that the Bottom Block (a wing in the local hospital, for the mentally unsound) held a number of people with infinitely more capacity for retaining knowledge than I had. Little-used words ranking high on his oratorical spit-list were cretin, lunatic and imbecile; at one time or another most of us managed to be all of those. We presumed that his wife always got the better of the arguments because he was so belligerent.

I told my parents the good news about the prospective job, whereupon my mother engaged first gear, did some shoulder-shrugging while speaking to me with the thickness of the wall to another room between us – as mothers do sometimes when they're not happy with what you've just said to them. My father, only half listening, nodded disinterestedly and engaged neutral. It was he who had found me an interim job, labouring on Holroyd's farm across the way when he'd walked over one Friday night to pay our milk bill. This was the period following my ignominious release from the sheet metal firm that I've spoken about previously.

Mother had Sunday and most of Monday to wind up her quarrelling spring, which was a fairly large and heavy-duty one. Tony shouted across our dividing garden wall after his work had finished on Monday night, that I should go and see the gaffer at "The Quarry" the following morning. The Quarry was the local name given to Besom Hill Brickworks situated at the north east side of Sholver Moor on Ripponden Road, near to a small dice-throw of houses known as Grains Bar. The company manufactured common brick and land drains and left its workforce pretty well knackered at the end of each day.

Mother must have overheard Tony's speech and her tightly coiled spring began clicking over its ratchet until it was heading for overwind. When I mentioned the prospective job again to my mother just after tea had finished, the rapidly over-winding spring suddenly sprung. The bursting storm went something like this, 'After all I've done for you; ironed your shirts, kept you tidy, bought you new clothes, even though you should be buying your own now that you're working, this is what you go and do, manual work, huh, as if this family hasn't had enough of that.' All of that was perfectly true – there was probably a lot more that she did for me, extra spending money etc. My father took the coward's way out and with his newspaper vanished upstairs to the bathroom as the spring went "Poing". Mother carried on smoothly through the gears, 'I had hoped for better things for you, trying to keep you out of dirty work and into something with a future. Well, you'll see my lad; when you get older you'll wish you'd listened to my advice – you'll be sorry, don't come whinging to me.' I can feel the empathy from those whose mothers went to the same phraseology classes as our mum. After taking a few deep breaths to get a second wind she said something like, 'All this time and effort; I don't know what the world's coming too, I really don't. You do your best for them and what do they do? Well see if I care, it's your life, do what you want with it'. For the second time and finally she said, 'Don't come running to me.' In full flow our mother had much in common with the Winchester Rifle, in that she repeated herself several times during the course of hostilities. If our father was listening from upstairs – which he couldn't help but do – I knew that his eyebrows would be arched in an expression of resignation as he waited for the storm to pass.

If there were any real benefit from the busted spring, it was that the house would soon be as shiny as a new pin – it was always shiny, but a new pin was the deluxe version. Our mum could remonstrate better when she had a tin of Johnson's Lavender wax polish and a cleaning cloth in her hands.

Whenever Ginger our cat sensed that a dispute was on the cards, he used to go and sit outside on the coal-shed-cum-washhouse roof out of the firing line, unless it was raining – in that case I assume he went to practise his wailing with the cats on the farm across the way. He wasn't above a bit of bother mind you – a rub-off from living in our house. Many have been the times I've seen him sitting in his basket looking sorry for himself, covered in bits of crossed sticking plaster with blobs of ointment dotted about his head. On other occasions there would be great swathes of his fur missing and sometimes he walked as if he'd been down to the pub for a pint or two of brain balm.

'What do you think Harry?' Joe, the manager of the brickworks said to his foreman. It was Tuesday morning and I was standing in the brickworks office while both men were seated in front of the open fire drinking pint pots full of muddy-looking tea. Harry's pot was similar in colour to a disturbed rain puddle – when it was purchased it was probably white. Joe was a nice man, fifty-ish, short and slim with a ready smile. Harry the yard-boss was on the short side too and there the resemblance ended. Harry was as wide as he was tall and the only place he carried any fat was on his sandwiches. He had 'Don't mess with me' written all over him. When he wasn't hitting his thumb with a hammer somewhere, he maintained the firm's electrical appliances and machinery; the rest of his time was taken up in the company workshop, doing what you do when you've nothing to do.

Without smiling or looking at me Harry asked, 'Is your father Joe Lavisher or Norman?'

'Joe' I said. (The latter was my uncle). I was taken aback that he should know the senior male members of my family.

Harry said, 'He used to do a bit of boxing when we were kids; we were on the same boxing team at St. Stephen's Boys' Club.'

Harry still wasn't about to crack a smile. His revelation was something that I wasn't aware of, but it explained how my father was able to clip my ear so easily when I'd transgressed as a child.

Much like Neville Chamberlain, I was guilty of misinterpreting the agreement for 'Peace In Our House/Time' – the difference being that my mistake was made on a fairly regular basis, whereas he only made the one as far as I know.

Harry stood up and said, 'We'll give him a try Joe, if he isn't up to it, we can always throw him out'.

This time he smiled, as you do at a private joke. Only his lips moved, his eyes would have chilled boiling porridge. Without looking at me he walked out of the office and into the yard. I wasn't expecting him to pat me on the shoulder and say 'Only kidding lad'. Huh, even though I was young, green and relatively clean, there was little hope of that happening in that man's world.

Nobody had discovered a man's feminine side, mainly because there wasn't and still isn't one. It's a fragment in the imagination of the wittering classes. I can just imagine, on Saturday night in town, offering some bonehead your "feminine side", be he drunk or sober. I withdraw that statement; I can't imagine it.

The work required ones brain to slip into low gear at its earliest opportunity and was easy if monotonous, a process known as Carrying-Off. The task was to lift "green" bricks or pipes (land drains) from machines that mixed the powdered shale with water and compressed the resulting goo into either of the objects, and then stack them onto a battery-powered truck. They were then taken round to the kiln for firing (baking) into the end product. The job in the brick-sheds was dirty and oily, particularly hard on clothing. One had to work for two weeks just to buy new clothing to replace the ones being used in your new job. Protective clothing was on offer.

'Got any safety-wear or protective clothing then?'

'Ay, go to th'office and they'll give you some rubber gloves and a bit of advice, we want the gloves back if you leave.'

On hot windy days the dust blew around the buildings – reminiscent of the North African sirocco that lifts the desert sand into impenetrable veils – colouring everyone's skin a darker shade of pale. Men went about their work like apparitions blending in well with the blackened walls of the brickyard buildings.

'Oops, didn't see you there Tom, was that your foot I just ran over with the truck; need some new boots (or new toes) now then, eh?'

On days like those, you could walk across Ripponden Road and look over the dry-stone wall towards Shaw. Low in the distance the town pulsed like an angry black heart. Its factory chimneys would belch out embryonic acid rain, the smoke surging and swelling as it strove to gain height for its long journey to Scandinavia, where it would sct about dccimating the pine forests of Norway. At cruising level the smoke lay flat in ever-thickening and darkening layers, before drifting towards the north-east, perhaps hoping to drop in on Newcastle or later touching Edinburgh where it would shorten their daylight hours considerably before crossing the North Sea.

It wasn't always like that of course. On still, sunny mornings the view was much clearer, a sharply defined skyline with its rounded, green-tinged hills stretching into the distance way beyond Rochdale, although the landscape wasn't of the type to have caused John Constable to trip over his easel, in a mad rush for his palette and brush. The view was pleasing as it radiated in warm, bright sunlight.

Ripponden Road, in common with most main roads at the time, was relatively traffic-free in the early morning. These days there are so many cars travelling down the road towards Oldham I'm reminded of discarded peas popping down the plug hole when the washing-up's finished after tea. (I tentatively suggested one day that we buy a dishwasher, but that was sidestepped with the comment, 'What for, when we already have one, you can't expect to do nothing for the rest of your life').

On days when I decided to walk from home up Ripponden Road to work, I had an uninterrupted view of Beal Valley (before the Sholver estates had been built) and could see the small cluster of houses at the hamlet known as Doghill near Grains Bar. During breakfast-break on calm, still days I sat outside the canteen and could hear the faint clatter of cotton-mill machinery; their windborne sounds drifting up the valley from Shaw and passing over my head to be absorbed against the quarry face. On days when the air was perfectly still, there was an intermittent droning from propeller-driven aircraft drifting on the wind's gentle up-draughts; silence reigned again once the aircraft had slipped through a hole in the sky somewhere over North Manchester.

Towards the autumn of the year, as I was about to enter the brickworks yard, I could see the sky low in the east blushing pink above a narrow band of pale violet. I've no idea what caused the effect, the thin band ran along the broken moorland horizon, dropping out of sight as it meandered behind the pitch and putt golf course before reappearing and heading for the rugged ground at High Moor. The band disappeared as the skyline continued on to the many overlapping ridges in the direction of Cheshire.

Peeping eagerly around the chimney stack of Doorstones Farm, the low sun would often make warm promises that it might not be able to keep for all of the day. Long shafts of sunlight stretched outwards from Bishop's Park on the hilltop at Grains Bar, lighting up the shale on a disused part of the quarry-face, turning the different strata into ochre and black stripes. Many-hued droplets glittered in the warming sun as morning dew danced across the shale in front of the probing fingers of light. (Shale is thin, hard, brittle, layered clay that forms over millennia near the earth's surface). Breezes hissed softly around the natural-stone buttressing along the quarry's upper ridge, plaguing the grassy overhangs that seemed to be waiting patiently for the weight of next winter's snowfall to bring them crashing down. Occasionally, before work started, the quarry was deathly quiet, as if it was daring something to break its slumber. Light breezes lifted whorls of fine dust from around the kilns; dancing and swirling like ballroom dancers as they drifted amongst the long stacks of land-drains. When the yard was free of any material, stiffer breezes made small dust devils dart away across its cinder surface like phantom mice racing to keep an appointment with a prancing flautist. Occasionally the trickle of falling shale would break the silence and then clatter to a stop as if ashamed of itself for the disruption. In the distance a cow might be bawling about its lot, or the knitting needle clack of a train might be heard as it made its purposeful way through the railway sidings at Royton. Other times there were late rabbits scampering amongst the small piles of broken pipes, or a well-rested tramp heading off into the bright morning, answering the inexorable summons after spending a luxurious night on the floor of a warm empty chamber in the kiln. The owners of the brickworks frowned upon the practice of vagrants sleeping in the yard, but I know that Walter, one of the night-shift fire-stokers, had some sympathy for certain itinerants and woke them up with a cup of tea before sending them on their way.

The working day always started off the same way. Were you a chap of timid disposition or liked to have a few minutes' doze in the firm's canteen before starting work, your little journey into dreamland would be rudely terminated by Harry the foreman.

'Right lads', he'd bellow through the canteen window, shaking the putty loose and causing the ceiling whitewash to flake. The building's appointments got a double shock because he did the same thing after dinner. The call was followed by the usual mumbling and whinging as the workforce found its feet en mass.

On reflection, it would have made a nice change to hear him say, 'Would anyone like to start work this morning?' or 'Isn't it a lovely day, let's see if we can't make a few bricks this afternoon, shall we?'

It's odd how fate plays cards with your life. Not many years previously, as children, we had taken great delight in hurling stones from the top of the quarry onto the unsuspecting, unprotected heads of those I was about to start work with. At the time of my commencement with the company, it seemed prudent to say nothing of this early defect in my character. Some fairly hefty men worked there, particularly the two lads who pushed the large "shale-tubs" up the railway lines to the quarry face to be filled. The company also employed a particularly large individual named Sid – said to have been in the Royal Marines – who sported a very short haircut and had muscles where most men have wishes. He worked in the drawing chambers (wheeling the hot, baked, bricks and land-drains outside from the newly opened chambers in the kiln). He was a pleasant enough chap to get on with, with a high-pitched London accent. I suppose you'd say he was quiet; however he hadn't followed his army career or got his muscles from growing petunias or practising origami. The thought of my much-loved torso, along with the shale, being dropped into the crushing pan (a revolving plate with huge rolling millstones), after a confession of stone throwing, was something that I didn't dwell on for too long. The resulting bricks would have given a rather different meaning to the phrase 'The house that Dave built'.

I was to leave my employment with the brickyard for the never-ending joys of working for the road mending section of the West Riding of Yorkshire County Council. I've never laughed as much as I did, or been as trouble-free as I was, in my whole life, throughout the following long, hot summer. However that's for later.

20

Around mid-summer in 1960, Terry whom I've mentioned previously, worked for the plastics firm Pakamac. Arnold his workmate had said, if we'd nothing better to do on Monday nights, we all ought to visit his village youth club in Denshaw. After a lot of whinging and talk of country-bumpkins, straw-chewers and grazer-gazers (pretty rich when we lived on the edge of the Lancashire prairies) we said we'd give it a go and turned up at the youth club.

I should explain a little about the village in those days. Denshaw is a mile or so over the county border in West Yorkshire. It is small and situated a couple of miles south of the junction 22 exit on the M62 motorway. In my time it boasted a church, one school, five pubs, one chip shop (which opened in the evenings – if the owners felt like opening it), a Post Office and a Co-operative Society store with butcher's shop combined. It gave shelter to one under-worked resident police constable, one reservoir waterman – who had some pecuniary interest in the chip shop and one psychotic Great Dane guard dog that scared the daylights out of anyone wishing to use the ladies' public conveniences. It did that by lying low and then barking its head off at any woman using the toilet entrance immediately next to its abode. The pooch lived in a large kennel in the back yard of the Junction Inn and took its responsibilities seriously. There will have been times when the purpose of a visit to the conveniences has occurred prematurely due to the dog's vigilance.

Situated on one side of the village crossroads was an institution rejoicing under the title of The Oddfellows club, which at weekends would be occupied by the odd fellow – stands to reason I suppose. In the dim and distant past, I've played cards and filled my tank in there until the cockerel has bellowed for his breakfast – resident constable or not. Prior to my joining the club's membership ranks a few years later – an arrangement that lapsed in the first moon of winter – I had thought that the association would be a much-diluted version of the Masons, embracing the same sort of rigmarole that surrounds their doings. I can remember speculating vividly about the wearing of goat masks and chanting my way round the snooker table upstairs, or perhaps you had to walk through doorways backwards with a colander on your head, whistling the theme tune from Dr. Zhivago. I can't remember the subscription fees or the acceptance ceremony when the time for my induction came around. Whatever the case, I was given to understand that there were many financial benefits to be had by becoming a member, like assistance when ill or with spectacles, stuff like that, it's probably a relic from the past when money was hard to come by. My joining The Oddfellows was probably pre-ordained anyway; they don't come much odder than me – or so I'm told.

There were a couple of restaurants and a sprinkling of farms on the edges of the village, the farms being made up mainly of pasture or grazing land, as are most of the farms in Saddleworth. The outer edges of the villages are topped off with rugged moorland and peat beds. Hillsides in Saddleworth are especially beautiful when the purple heather blooms on their middle to upper reaches.

The Co-operative Society building on Ripponden Road Denshaw played host to the youth club. The premises were entered via a narrow wooden covered staircase, leading upstairs to the large wooden-floored hall, which in turn led to two smaller rooms. There were stairs at the far end of the large room going down to a cellar, which was home to some weight-lifting gear for the youth club's use. I don't know who supplied the equipment. The large room must originally have been a community room; there was a piano and some staging to hold pantomimes and other social pastimes – on winter nights perhaps. The place smelled dustily old fashioned but not unpleasantly so, with its tall windows, half wood-panelling walls and a high ribbed ceiling. You could buy drinks and crisps at a reasonable price and a record player was in constant use by the kids. The acoustics were excellent in the main room; music seemed to squirrel its way around the high ceiling beams and bounce off the tops of the long windows. The youth club was organised by two local men, Don Pemberton, a stonemason by trade; I don't know what Bill Womersley did for a living. When the youth club closed for the evening, everyone congregated on the cobbled frontage of the Junction Inn down in the village, making a lot of noise and generally being a damn nuisance – that's what Roy the pub's landlord said anyway. The village chip shop wasn't of much use to us, to the owners, or to their bank manager; on the nights that we fancied some chips it was usually closed.

A few years later I was to live in the village for a short time. At weekends there, apart from shadows, nothing much moved before

10a.m., particularly on Sundays. The main signs of life were the constant squawking of rooks nesting in the large trees at the junction's five-road split. There was the occasional visitor to McLintock's newspaper shop-cum-Post Office at the same crossroads. Ah, yes I almost forgot! There were regular visits from a large black dog that came to apply a few fluid ounces of paint stripper to the base of the Corporation lamp post outside Mrs Henthorn's house on the opposite corner to the rookery.

To continue with the original theme. We knew after that first night at the youth club that the fire brigade wouldn't be required to attend while the evening was in progress; the place wasn't going to catch fire owing to any fireworks that might go off under its roof. We discussed the matter on the bus going home. The dialogue went something along the lines of, 'Won't be going there again, wadda dump that was.' You'll gather that it wasn't an in-depth discussion requiring sagacity or great powers of deduction. In fact, with most of his brain power for the day still unused, one of the lads chewed his bus ticket until it was wet through, unscrewed a light bulb on the curvature of the bus's side wall where it met the roof, stuck the soggy bus ticket into the light socket and screwed the bulb back into its place. The hope was that in doing so it would fuse all the lights on the bus when they were switched on later in the evening. He was quite inventive in his own field was our lad, although to his credit he wasn't into graffiti.

We persevered a second week at the youth club, but the requirement for teenage stimulation was not met for some of us. After that, the nucleus of our group disbanded – that was it, all done. What made that situation even more odd was that we all lived within spitting distance of each other, on the same street. Lawrie had been doing some serious courting with Kath the girl that he eventually married. He and his family emigrated to Australia and Kath joined them some months later. I've no idea what eventually became of Terry, Bob and latterly Roger, the other recalcitrant youths in our outfit.

I went to Denshaw Youth Club on the third week, on my own. During our visit the previous week I had made a nodding acquaintance with a lad named Alan and sought him out as the first port of call while trying to work out how things shook down in the new environment.

The village was Christmas-card pretty in winter and particularly quiet on winter nights. Buses were infrequent to non-existent when snow was on the ground. North Western ran a single-deck bus service that turned around in the village and went back as it came, via Delph to wherever its depot was. Oldham Corporation ran a bus service via Grains Bar and periodically, perhaps hourly, a Yorkshire bus company (the service was referred to as the Express) ran through the village towards Oldham from Ripponden and returned. In mid-winter, passage through the snow-filled roads was largely dependent upon Alf Hall being able to get his Caterpillar D.8 bulldozer through the snow. Alf was a heavy-plant contractor based in Delph village. There was difficulty attached to his operations because people abandoned their cars as the roads filled in, leaving Alf or one of his drivers to push them unknowingly into the field walls that lined the roadside. When the snow was beginning to melt, the roadside often looked like a repository for squashed, extra-large tin cans. Brand-named tins of course, Ford, Wolseley, Jaguar, Daimler, they all looked pretty much the same when the bulldozer had finished with them.

Alan, who lived at Watersheddings on the outskirts of Oldham, and I had decided to walk to Denshaw one blowy, snowy night around January – just to see what height the snowdrifts over the hills had achieved. We were surprised to see traffic running downhill from Grains Bar towards Oldham and wondered how this could be, when snow was starting to drift across the roads and against the field walls. Setting off down the long and twisty incline that leads to Denshaw, we walked in tyre tracks that were slowly filling in on the snow-packed road surface. Snow was of the fine type, resembling fine mesh as it swept through the orange light of the main road lamps, blowing in huge swirls like high surf at Hout Bay on the African Cape. Loud crackling and hissing noises came from overhead power lines, covered with frozen snow and hanging dangerously low from great spidery pylons that seemed to march from Crompton Moor, across the top of the Tame Valley before tramping off over High Moor. Approaching the first bend in the road before the Golden Fleece public house, we saw the dim, practically useless, headlight beams of a Land Rover, which was towing a car out of the mini-blizzard. Closer inspection of the vehicle revealed young Roger Townson and his half frozen mate – trussed up like two Eskimos – piloting the Land Rover; there was a big smile on Roger's snow encrusted face as he drove by, as happy as a pig outside a derelict bacon factory. I think Roger's dad founded Townson Tankers (petroleum carriers) around that time. Whether Roger did the good deed of towing for gain or just for the hell of it I don't know. When we eventually got to Denshaw village it was closed. It wasn't boarded up or anything like that – it was just closed.

The preoccupation with town or area twinning, pursued with some vigour by our local authorities in the seventies, could quite easily have been met for Saddleworth during winter months, by sticking a pin anywhere in a map of Siberia

Not long after Alan and I became acquainted, some lads from Delph made an appearance at the club. The lads were considered to be undesirables by the two adults in charge of the club's affairs, who because of their great age obviously knew plenty about such things. Alan, plus a lad nicknamed Woody, and I had the somewhat dubious pleasure of asking them to leave, on the understanding that if they refused they would be thrown out on their collective ears. They left without so much as a whinge. The staircase leading down to the main road was quite narrow and completely boxed in with tongue and groove wood. Chucking someone down those stairs would have made a noise similar to that heard when a few golf balls find their way into a clothes-drying machine and the machine is switched on. He was a great lad Alan, easy-going, but not to be fooled with if you weren't equipped to repel boarders. The family home was in Carlton Avenue, Watersheddings until his dad bought Addison's pet store and fishing tackle shop in High Street, Lees. His mum, dad and sisters were some of the nicest people you could wish to meet. I think Alan worked in heavy-plant repairs, apprenticed to George Dew's. A number of kids from the Youth Club went horse riding from Enid Holmes' Riding Stables at the old Print Works yard in Denshaw on Saturday afternoons. Alan seemed to be running the show in Enid's absence and rode the horses that nobody else would ride, either because the horse had a bad temperament or was loaded up with equine exuberance. We drank a bit of beer and hung around the village dances for a while until some situation or other prompted a move-on. (Probably a girl appeared on the scene). Alan became a policeman – for which he has been forgiven – and later a detective working from Chadderton Police Station.

It's a much-nurtured hope amongst policemen that they be guaranteed a place in heaven; if that is the case they will have to enter by the back door. They won't be able to get in the front door for politicians, solicitors, drug dealers and gangsters all trying to bribe their way in.

21

We spent some of our time at the Youth Club downstairs, fooling around with weightlifting equipment. During one of those comedy half hours a young lady and her friends came downstairs to observe our efforts. I should mention that I was to weightlifting what Arnold Schwarzenegger is to weight watching, I had difficulty lifting a weight off my mind never mind anything else. Before Arnold, an American named Charles Atlas was the world's most perfectly built man, whose development lads were supposed to try and achieve. Apparently he was so big, he was to be declared America's 50th State, but they decided that Hawaii was the better option because it came with Hula girls and flowers. I could see that the girls weren't overly impressed with my prowess because they spent a lot of time laughing – sometimes until they hiccoughed. They followed that humbling experience with periods of arm nudging and noisily ran up and down the cellar stairs, presumably to see if I'd expired during their last period of absence. It's possible they were taking bets on my acquiring a hernia before the Youth Club finished for the day, I never did find out. Eventually the first young lady reached out, as I was removing some weights from the lifting bar that my groin wasn't happy with and with a good, firm, tug removed a large chunk of my hair. I didn't yelp although the pain was a killer. She must have mistakenly thought I was a bit of a tough guy. The relationship took off from that point hurtling into the unknown unchecked, as these things often do.

If anyone knows the whereabouts of that lock of hair, I could do with it back. These days the skin on my forehead has stretched a fair bit. Our bathroom comb and I have been negotiating its semi-retirement package these last few years and I welcome any assistance in staving off that day. The girls lived in Delph, the next village along the valley; consequently they were classed as foreigners.

Delph is just a coin's flip from the edge of the A62 trunk road, which links Oldham to Huddersfield and lies equidistant from both. There is a link road connecting all the villages in the area, the beginning of which runs from Denshaw at Saddleworth's northerly outpost through to Greenfield on its south-westerly border and is some five miles long, following faithfully the course of the fledgling River Tame. The village centre straddles the river and is comprised of a small number of "mixed" shops with cottages and terraced houses to their rear. There were and are two small council-owned estates tagged onto the upper part of the village. Three churches served the immediate village along with four public houses, Delph Band Club, the Reform Club and the Mechanics' Institute, which provided the venue for other social activities. (I'm not sure if the theatre group existed at the time). A cricket and bowling club and the village football team made up the sporting side of things. The village housed an Urban District Council highways yard and a West Riding of Yorkshire council depot had recently been built on the outskirts of the village, the latter seeming more than anything else to be the home of two enormous, six wheeled, American 'Mack' Gritters with huge butterfly blades, (snowplough attachments). The blades spent the summer sunning themselves on a grass verge outside the depot situated on Delph New Road near to Delph crossroads. The village-centre buildings form a huddle under the lee of Delph Hill, which gives some shelter from the bitter, easterly winter winds that blow off Saddleworth Moor from the direction of Huddersfield. Lying in a valley basin, the village submerged when the West Yorkshire snow-chute opened around the month of January dumping large amounts of white stuff on it. Beside themselves with joy when that happened, east winds raced through the lanes and other access roads chasing snow high up the walls of buildings and high up anyone caught out on the streets.

I had arranged to meet my new girlfriend Elisabeth at the Youth Club on her home ground in Delph village. Not having been to the village before, I asked directions and was unsure of what to expect when I arrived at the club. Entering Delph Primary School I recall being met by the tune *Wonderful Land* by the Shadows. Elisabeth took me round and I was introduced to some of her friends, a courtesy that struck me as odd for those times and I recall feeling slightly embarrassed. (My being embarrassed was about as likely as a gourmet chef moonlighting in a transport cafe).

Delph Youth Club was a different set-up to the one at Denshaw and was as good a youth club as young folk could hope for. Someone brought in all the latest records of the time, *Let's Twist Again, The Locomotion, Have I The Right, Wonderful Land, Love Letters, Telstar*, and stuff like that. The lads could play five-a-side football in the main schoolroom using a purse-sized beanbag, or when the weather was fine and dry we used a proper football on the school football pitch outside at the rear of the building. The school was turned over to youth and older children, lock, stock and packets of crisps. A chap named Les Mingham ran the Youth Club. He was a truly nice man, always finding time to listen to the kids and we should have been grateful to him at the time. Like nearly everything else in life that's good, it's usually appreciated in retrospect. If anyone deserved recognition for his endeavours on behalf of the youth of the village it was Les Mingham. I say this without any thought other than that the man was tireless in his pursuits on youth's behalf and had the patience of a one-armed man chasing peas around his dinner plate. Along with the Youth Club, Les ran the village football team and organised the occasional Saturday night dances.

At the time they were held upstairs in the Reform Club (Delph Club as it's now known) on Gartside Street, Delph. Later venues for the dances were the Independent Church Hall at Hillend Road or the Youth Club, which by this time was being held in the old canteen next to Delph Primary School. Word got around about the dances and their attendant pop groups; young people came from Shaw and Oldham, others came from as far away as Rochdale. Later-to-become-famous groups such as The Hollies, Mike Cadillac and the Playboys and the Rockin' Vicars entertained at the dances.

A couple of lads associated with the Rimmon Mountaineering Club turned up at the dances, presumably because there isn't much call for rock climbing in the dark hours. I've never been sure of the climbers' exact social standing in the community although I do recall that some weren't doing much standing on evenings over the weekend. Those two lads worked on the theory that drinking six pints of bitter entitled them to seek their own forms of entertainment, usually by punching the nearest dancing male or sometimes the one just standing next to them in the hall. Jumping up and down on a dance floor is not a good place to be, when someone wishes you to see stars without the benefit of removing the roof. The bother-causers eventually found their match in the shape of a lad named Bill, who had recently come to live on the outskirts of the village and nurtured a very good line in head-beating and general disablement of the limbs. Not someone you would fool around with when he was wound up. When he was not in combative mood he seemed a right-enough bloke to me.

Elisabeth and I sometimes went for walks up the Tame Valley. The river burbled softly as it dropped to lower levels on its way down the valley, pooling on gently sweeping bends where fingerling trout darted for cover at our approach. Tall, pollen-covered grasses swayed to the rhythm of unseen pulses and light breezes played in the crown of the large oak tree at the rear of Pingle Mill, pushing its branches into conformation as we neared the wooden footbridge. The tree's lower, swishing, branches seemed to be whispering amongst themselves, as if they knew something that they didn't want me to know. Swallows skimmed across the river's surface, swooping upwards when approaching the footbridge before turning to arrow round and do the run again. We could hear distant cries from children playing on the old tennis courts on Pingle Lane while other children could be found teetering on stones or wading in the river's shallows under the King Street road bridge in their endless quest to spot trout.

(You'll have to forgive me when the prose gets a little flowery – sometimes I forget who the person was that I'm supposed to be describing). If time was plentiful we'd walk up to Delph Heights counting sheep, discussing the theory behind crop rotation or estimating the tonnage of hay produced from one meadow – you'll know how it goes I'm sure. Someone at Higher Barn Farm was building a boat at the side of his home. The partly-built boat was erected on large wooden stilts, the stilts being of a robust nature because the boat was in the Scandinavian Ferry class – maybe that's a small exaggeration. I used to wonder how – if the craft were ever to achieve maturity – it was going to find its way to a body of water sufficient for it to sail upon. The lanes are very narrow in that area and not well made, making it difficult for a large boat or anything much bigger than a cartload of hay to be transported easily. Perhaps the boat builder was a Noah-type who was waiting for the tides of wrath to descend upon us, in which case he and his would be sitting high and dry. The water required to float the blessed thing would have had to be more than a few bucketsful before the craft would rise from its staging. The Ark sat on its framework in semi-neglected splendour for many years. I suppose that it was something gaze-worthy when all our previous options were exhausted.

Once or twice we walked up Delph Lane past the football pitch and along the road past the Mousery to the beginning of Castleshaw Camp Road or Waterworks Road to use its proper name. I assume the Mousery business bred mice for experimentation purposes and it wasn't a bid to deprive the area of cheese, or to keep mousetraps in full employment in some of the old properties abounding on the hillsides. Maybe some of the mice were released to give the village cats something to do when they got fed up with wearing out the hearthrug. At the other end of Waterworks Road is Castleshaw Camp School, beyond the school lie the two Castleshaw Reservoirs. The distant bleating of sheep broke the rural stillness as we trod the swampy path by the brook upon our return to the village. If the hour was fairly late there was a chance that you would hear bleating from the lesser-legged beer slurper as he sought a return to the tree he had fallen out of earlier in the evening on his way to the pub.

Viewed from Castleshaw, some of the sunsets over Grains Bar were of the deep-red, blacksmith's furnace type, from the edge of which long silver and golden streaks reached out towards the east in welcome to the imminent arrival of night. They were great blazing affairs like huge gas fires turned up a notch or two more than the evening chill merited. At other times the skies appeared to have been sprayed with a soft-amber blush and were cloud-wisped with long cuttings of furled lace. The cotton clouds nearest the sun were edged sharply with the finest of crimson lines, they seemed reluctant to leave the area stretching along the hilltops like whitecaps on the sea before dissipating slowly until they fused with the violet of the approaching darkness.

Skies of that kind usually herald the onset of autumn, unlike Jerry Keller who optimistically sang *Here Comes Summer* throughout the year's later months. Still, it was youth's own song at the time even if it was a bit mushy compared with today's romance-free offerings.

I sometimes wonder if that famed enchantress Rose Tinted turns up in her glasses and waves her wand about when I remember personal moments. I was just comparing those times with today's idea of a romantic evening. I understand from listening to today's youth that their version of a romantic hour or two is a visit to their chosen hostelry, sample every drink that is on display and mix some of their own when they've run out of brand names. After closing time at the pub, they have a loud singing-do or a five-street argument on the way to Whin Gin Gut's the local oriental restaurant. If it's raining, they pay a visit to Yer So Dim's the nearby English chip shop and remove a couple of gallons of curry and chips from its premises, thereafter waiting patiently until the early hours of morning when the first signs of illness begin to appear. Ah, such joy! I wish I were eighteen again.

You can get into love trouble with a girl, under those circumstances that I mentioned earlier – and of course I did. I can't remember any big musical score accompanying the time we had together, but we had our own songs, the drums of youth beat softly in easy tempo and we had gentle moments.

Songs of the time were *Sealed with a Kiss*, Brian Hyland; *I Love How You Love Me*, The Paris Sisters; *I Remember You*, Frank Ifield; *Please Don't Ever Change*, The Crickets; *Speedy Gonzales*, Pat Boone; *Let There Be Drums*, Sandy Nelson; *Tell Me What He Said*, Helen Shapiro and *When My Little Girl Is Smiling*, Craig Douglas. All overly sentimental songs by today's standards I suppose. Matters could have been worse; we could have had our youth in the Punk or Rap era (I seem to have missed a letter out near the end of that sentence). That would have been thrilling, I'm sure.

22

Around that time I changed my work allegiance from the brickworks to the West Riding of Yorkshire County Council – not to be confused with Saddleworth U.D.C.

It was to be one of the more amusing partnerships in my life.

The roads' maintenance section was based in a scruffy shambles of a yard, at the bottom of Millgate next to Delph crossroads. The collection point for workers waiting to be ferried to the outer reaches of the district was on the footpath outside the wall-enclosed yard. The U.D.C. operation was run from a small office and a couple of storage sheds or garages within the yard. The depot was eventually given a long overdue makeover (it was filled in) and is now a steep grass verge opposite the bus stop on Millgate – or The Sound, as it's known. The new offices, vehicle workshop and messing facilities were situated across the A62 road next to the salt yard that faced onto Delph Station sidings on Dobcross New Road. I was to work in one of the road gangs and knew a few of its members already, fitting into the road crew fairly easily. Working hours began at 7.30am; I was already knackered before we started, having to run from Moorside to Delph, the bus service from Oldham being subject to attacks of disorientation when asked to go beyond Waterhead. An open truck with shallow sides pulled up – on hire from a chap in the village – and we all piled onto the back. We sat like a bunch of skittles inside a large aluminium shelter that was off-loaded on arrival at the stretch of road we were about to resurface. The road needing our attention at the time was a strip of road outside the Olive Branch pub in Marsden, a small village in the Colne Valley situated on the main A62 road to Huddersfield. While on the subject of the aluminium shelter, it wasn't always tied down to the floor of the truck, the premise being that if we were all sitting on the wooden bench-seats inside it, the lightweight shelter couldn't fly off the truck. However, you know how it is; the day's been scorching and the vehicle is returning you to the depot at night; nobody wants to sit inside the shelter because it's like the inside of a hot oven, so they sit outside on the floor or sides of the truck to face the cooling breeze. I recall when the shelter made a bid for freedom after the truck had negotiated Standedge Cutting, heading towards the Floating Light public house down the hill. The shelter gave no hint that it was about to dismount from the truck, not even a practice hop. Imperceptibly the thing inched backwards until it was enough into the wind to fill its sails and then it made a scuffling leap into the air. Amid frantic shouts of 'Whoa' and 'Grab the bloody thing', the driver applied his brakes quickly, whereupon the shelter, numerous bodies, a few empty lunch bags, flasks, picks, shovels and any road mending paraphernalia that were present on the truck, immediately shot forward forming a large pile. Legs and arms had to be untangled and restored to their rightful owners; scrapes and bruises were shown around like medals from a war. Selected words – not ones used in public discourse – were given a thoroughly good workout with plenty of shoulder shrugging thrown in to emphasis certain viewpoints. Embarrassed strutting took place up and down the roadside while older men wearing flat caps, vigorously batted dust from their clothing using the caps as beaters. Indignation was sprayed around like visitors using the free testers at the Fragonard perfume factory in Grasse, Sud de France. When all the aggression, swearing and steam had been vented thoroughly, our journey continued. The aluminium shelter was now packed to seating capacity, while every now and again small spasms of squeaky, nervous laughter slipped out from its dark interior. Life was great, verging on the hysterical for quite a while after that. Frankie Thorpe (a workmate) and I laughed until the wax pinged from our ears whenever the incident was mentioned. I have often thought that uncontrollable laughter when one is young can be quite life threatening. There have been times when the outpouring of laughter has not been matched by my intake of oxygen, causing distress to internal organs and astonishment to anyone watching my face suffuse into a wonderful shade of blue. Allied to that of course is the replacement of gallons of tears. I have found the nearest hostelry to be a good source of replenishment when my mirth tank runs dry.

The road gang was made up of two separate teams, one arriving from a depot at Elland, near Huddersfield, at roughly the same time that we arrived from the one at Delph. Working relations were pretty harmonious between the gangs, although the other gang didn't half speak funnily. If there was a problem, it was that each gang had its own ganger (foreman). The chap in charge of the Saddleworth contingent was named Bill who looked as if many a good meal had passed him by. He was uncommonly gifted with apathy, distressingly on the slim side and terminally cheerful with it. Bill had never been invited to a Temperance Society Meeting, consequently he viewed anything liquid in a glass, in a pub, including the flower vases, as fair game for consumption. Every dinnertime he was mightily burdened with a need to visit the pub from which he often didn't return until 4.00p.m. in time for the 'load-up' – if he returned at all.

Bill's counterpart from Elland was nicknamed Bud (he was so named because rather than remember everyone's name he called them "Bud"). Bud was around five feet eight inches tall with white hair and he was quite rotund. When The Lord was handing out waistlines Bud drew a fairly large one. I expect he was standing in the Sumo wrestlers' queue by mistake. He packed away sixteen stone or so in weight under his weskit and voluminous, brown, corduroy trousers. On top form he could have shouted down a Member of Parliament without raising his voice. Sometimes, disconcertingly, in the middle of one of his orations a loud rumbling noise issued from deep down in his lard-covered diaphragm. Belly gurgling is distracting to say the least, when an employee is trying to follow instructions from his superior, sometimes producing an involuntary snigger in the worker. The half-muffled merriment seemed to whiz past Bud's monolithic outline without the slightest trace of embarrassment on his part. Even so, in his high-profile capacity as the representative of The West Riding of Yorkshire Highways' Maintenance Department, Bud was not to be trifled with by a person not protected by the authority's umbrella.

The A62 road was the main thoroughfare into Lancashire from Yorkshire at the time and was continually in use by large goods-carrying companies such as Hanson, Peter Slater and Smith and Robinson. The latter were a trucking company which employed many, large, multi-wheeled liquid-carrier tankers in their everyday activities. One of Smith and Robinson's tanker drivers took it upon himself to fall foul of Bud not long after I took up employment on the road gangs. It was a mistake. I've never thought that the driver's initial indiscretion was premeditated, more a spur of the moment thing that got out of hand. Whatever. He must have decided that there was satisfaction to be gained on a regular basis when he took a spoon to the wrath of Bud and began stirring it around a bit. I still wonder if he was up amongst the stars, drinking jungle-juice or inhaling some form of opiate when he decided upon the course of action that he was about to take. How else can one explain why the chap started taking uninhibited delight in running his tanker's wheels over the long line of rubber cones separating the road workings from the road in use, causing them to leap into the air and scatter? Not long after the first incidence of the man's new found pleasure, Bud started pouring fuel into his personal wrath-meter until eventually it reached the brim. At that point, Bud became incandescent with rage, jumping up and down like a firewalker with blisters, spitting out loose fillings and epithets with equal ferocity. Our foreman nearly burst a blood vessel, when, after shaking his fist and yelling at the driver, the man shoved his arm out of his lorry window and gave Bud the 'Victory' sign in passing. When the burst dam that was the remnants of his temper had finally drained away, Bud wrote down the registration number of the vehicle when it was brought to a halt by our temporary traffic lights. Roughly a week after the first incident the vehicle had become familiar enough for him to recognise it clearly. Bud was biding his time, knowing the vehicle was never loaded for its return journey from Lancashire because of the bonging noise coming from its empty tank when it rode roughshod over his road cones. The coned-off area was roughly two hundred yards long or maybe a bit more. Seeing the vehicle brought to a stop at the traffic lights one day, Bud sauntered casually to the other end of the workings from that where the tanker was waiting. He checked that three large pieces of concrete were still hiding underneath three slightly larger-than-normal road cones, consecutively placed towards the end of the line. With an air of expectancy we all stopped work to watch the show once the tanker got under way. Presumably, the driver, thinking he had a captive audience thought it was Showtime too and ran his tanker right along the row of cones as usual. Nearing the end of the line of cones and because of stubbornness by the concrete lumps with their refusal to be crushed, one side of the tanker leapt into the air causing its rear end to fishtail sideways. In its vigorous efforts to stay upright, the tanker skittled the mobile traffic lights, which were stationed there and looking in the opposite direction. Righting itself, the vehicle clipped Yorkshire Frank's J.C.B, parked across the end of the workings, with its loading bucket resting on the road and full of new kerbs. The truck's momentum brought its rear end round in a semi-circle where it came to rest near the nose of the driver of the first car in line, waiting to go in the opposite direction. I'll bet the tanker driver's insurers gave a distant empathic shudder as the rear wheels of the large vehicle came to rest near the head of the terrified car driver. Silence reigned for a while, until the driver shot out of his cab. I can tell you he wasn't singing a passage from Verdi's Rigoletto as he inspected the rear end of his tanker. There were vague similarities in his enunciation, volume and pitch as he scuttled around his vehicle like a ferret in a rabbit warren. In the final tally of things broken, he found a badly crumpled mudguard, a deflated tyre and its damaged rim, a shattered taillight cluster and a torn hosepipe used in the transfer of liquid from the tanker into whichever receptacles it made deposits. Oh yes, his amusement portfolio was going to need something of an overhaul too.

The driver started doing a bit of finger wagging in the general direction of Bud's nose. Bud wasn't having any of that though, you could tell by the prominent edges appearing on his jutting jaw. I'm fairly sure I heard the sound 'Grrr' issuing from deep within Bud's well-padded gut. Unusual as it was to witness it, Bud smiled. Lifting his arms and shoulders in that classic Italian show of innocence, he stuck out his belly and said, 'You wer goin' too fast mate, you need to be a bit more careful with yer drivin''. From then onwards and as far as I recall, the traffic cones lived an undisturbed existence, except for the odd excursion by a beer-propelled car driver navigating his way into the deeper secrets of road excavation during the dark hours.

Disaster made an unwelcome appearance one day when a small van carrying Asian workers to their nightly toil was rolling along the A62 at a fairly good lick of speed. The van was at the head of a small procession, which comprised a high-sided, 22 tonne, loose-coal truck fully loaded, a half dozen cars with an empty bus bringing up the tail. The cavalcade was heading towards Marsden in the direction of Saddleworth and fast approaching our diggings at the Olive Branch pub – it was mid to late afternoon. If memory serves me correctly the men in the van were going to their employment in the Saddleworth Woollen Mills. The traffic lights changed to red against the flow and the van driver applied his vehicle's brakes at the very last minute (or so the coal truck driver said) causing the truck to hit the van and the cars to run into the back of each other. The empty bus was just a spectator. We all downed tools and ran to see if we could assist those trapped in the van. The coal truck had pushed the van and its contents ten yards or so up the road, killing the two passengers tucked down behind the rear seat and seriously injuring four men sitting on the unsecured back seat of the seven hundredweight van. The van driver had serious chest injuries from his unexpected clash with the van's steering wheel. His front-seat passenger, curiously the non-working boss of the other men – he just went with them to make sure they got on with their work – was unhurt. When we arrived at the scene, people just kept popping out of the van; it was like watching a magician pulling items from a hat. The Fire Brigade arrived to cut the two unlucky ones from behind the crushed rear doors of the van, using hacksaws and what appeared to be some type of heavy double-jawed axe. Two policemen turned up and filled numerous pages of their little black books prior to one of them sending traffic back from whence it had come. The one requiring a statement from me was Bunteresque, the other one, shouting himself into a lather about nosey motorists, looked and sounded as if he ate stone chippings with his morning cereals. The barely-scratched coal truck was driven to one side of the road and later collected by a heavy recovery unit, presumably for later inspection by the police. Two hours later there was no sign of an accident except for a nearly-dry oil patch on the road, which we'd covered with sand. It was as if the wind had arrived and blown the accident away. I was delegated to sweep the sand and broken glass into the road diggings. Living near to the scene of the incident these days and passing the spot regularly, I waste a fair bit of time wondering if that glass is still holding up the road surface and what happened to most of the participants in that cameo in my life.

Today the accident would be a full day of a job from start to conclusion. People would be dancing around waving clipboards, hundreds of metres of coloured tape would be wrapped around lampposts and trees and probably you, if you stood still near the scene for any length of time. Twenty-five-year-old 'Experts' would appear, fully briefed on every subject from the position of the sun at the moment of vehicle impact to the decomposition of the tarmac after a winter's gritting. Photographers would elbow you out of the way in their hope of winning the ghoulish Photograph of the Year award. Then of course there would be legions of lawyers, phalanxes of stress counsellors and waiting psychiatrists, all notifying bank managers of their imminent wealth and ready to carer-share those unfortunate enough to be involved.

The drivers made mistakes – so what, don't we all?

23

Elisabeth and I were invited to a number of parties over the Christmas period that year. One at Oxhey, Denshaw, I remember well. We had snow during the festivities and nobody was aware of it until it was time to go home. The lanes were filling in with drifting snow; lights in the village across the field were like soft glowing diamonds through a gossamer curtain in the fine sifting snow on the hilltop. Running along the valley top from Grains Bar towards Delph, dark undulating hilltops were just visible, as if someone had traced an ink-smeared finger across the middle of the sky.

It may sound tame in these days of alcohol consumption by school children, but there was little evidence of beer at these dos, except for the occasion when a lad from Denshaw produced a bottle of Cherry Brandy. He said he'd pinched it from his dad's drinks shelf, rearranging the bottles so that his appropriation wouldn't be easily spotted, intending to return the bottle at some later stage. With enthusiastic help from his mate, they reduced the contents of the bottle to a couple of tot glasses worth, over a period of two hours or so. After bouts of incoherent rambling, a common condition amongst youngsters learning how to buy or acquire a headache, he ran outside in a considerable sweat and released most of the liqueur over a field wall. His pal, wishing not to be left out of anything, followed him outside giving an almost perfect reproduction of his mate's accomplishment. While vomiting is not usually a spectator sport, it seems to attract a morbid interest in those not participating, more so when the purging is synchronized. The lads weren't aware or didn't care that they had a speculative audience – speculating whether death would be a consequence of their distress. They looked like negatives as they emerged from the snow, white faces giving a camouflage effect against the snow. I felt moved to applaud the production, quickly restraining myself after a look of censure from Elisabeth. Ask me what else we did at the parties and I couldn't tell you, other than playing records, eating and talking. Bedrooms were off limits for anything other than using the beds as coat hangers.

We were asked to a party at Tamecroft Farm, halfway up Grains Road on the right hand side, between Delph and Grains Bar. The uneven, unmade track down to the farm was also unlit. Bumping into one another, walking into rickety fencing and an occasional lashing from low tree branches was the order of the day – it was something of an obstacle course to reach the house. Friends from the Youth Club, whose parents had no qualms about leaving a dozen or so teenagers to their own devices, gave the party. The only thing I can remember about that occasion was having to, or choosing to, carry my girlfriend on my back most of the way home to Delph. Again, we had snow during the evening and she was wearing footwear designed to enhance the shape of her legs rather than help her bulldoze her way through twelve inches of drifting snow. Walking along the road you could see the far hillsides on the Friarmere side of the valley, which were lit by a sprinkling of street lamps, each one placed outside a far-flung property, be it farmhouse or cottage. From the lack of lighting between properties, the local authorities must have thought lane dwellers could see in the dark. Under freezing conditions the aureoles of soft light in a lamppost's immediate vicinity made the snow glitter like millions of tiny ampoules filled with quicksilver. It seemed as if someone had bored holes in a black sky to let discs of moonlight through.

Denshaw Youth Club provided seasonal activities around the village such as carol singing, for which we practised reluctantly over a period of a few weeks. It horrifies me still, when I think how I unconsciously made the transition from lad-about-town and ne'er-do-well to a person of reasonable respectability and worse still becoming a member of a communal warbling team. (The change didn't last long mind you).

We were invited first to sing carols at Cusick's house. They were a comfortably-off family who lived in a large detached dwelling on Oldham Road, Denshaw. The family and friends appeared to be in the middle of a serious singing session as we arrived at the bottom of their driveway. Once the show got under way we swiftly found ourselves drowned out by their strong choral presentation. It's probable that no one would have noticed if we had shut up altogether and let them get on with it. The family were good to us and gave us some kind of refreshment, I can't remember what it was – so it wasn't alcohol. Finishing there, we sang in the Junction Inn, The Black Horse, the Spinners Arms and the Oddfellows Club. After that we went to Mrs. Henthorn's house situated on the five-way crossroads. After doing a couple of numbers we were offered a light supper. Mrs Henthorn was a nice lady. We learned later that some in our company, sitting behind the settee, ate the contents of a small half-full box of chocolates, pushing the empty box under the settee when they'd finished. Apparently the chocolate-bereft box wasn't required until approaching New Year's Eve when somebody at the house fancied a chocolate and found the box to be missing (found the box to be missing?). When the club reconvened in the New Year, denials flew thick and fast and wide-eyed innocence made its first appearance of the year when the theft became the subject of an inquiry by Don the Youth Club leader. I know what you're thinking and I had nothing to do with it whatsoever. I knew who did, but like most people who conceal other peoples chocolate by eating it, I had no opinion on the matter. (My sister and I are life members of the chocolate-stealers club, having paid our dues early on in life). We were asked to contribute towards a replacement box of chocolates. I hadn't eaten them and so I didn't contribute. I pay my taxes with some reluctance and only then because the wallpaper in our house is considerably more appealing than that which decorates the insides of Strangeways Prison.

24

Some of the local lads were not happy to see me when I first ventured into Delph village. Are they ever, with comers-in who may be taking a resource out of the gene pool? That became apparent when my new girlfriend and I went into Hilda's chip shop on King Street. Upon entering the shop one of two clowns put his foot behind the door when I tried to open it. A vigorous shove caused the door to fly open, catching the obstructive one full in the face.

'Oops' and a smirk, an offering not intended to pacify. The two seemed displeased but neither commented, maybe they were unhappy because the girl was pretty and with the wrong man. Still, they weren't choosing, she was – I didn't care anyhow.

We both asked Hilda for 'A dose'. (The term is not to be confused with that which ladies of ill-repute sometimes distribute amongst their clientele or that which doctors prescribe for ill people). 'A dose' was teenage vernacular for chips and mushy peas with a teaspoonful of salt and an eggcup's worth of vinegar in a small grease-proofed bag. Hilda wrapped the purchase expertly in a single page of *The Yorkshire Post*, sticking a small wooden fork inside to be used as masher-cum-utensil once outside the premises.

There were separate factions of lads in the village. The first group that I met were your regular, conventionally dressed, football and cricket playing types, most with girlfriends from within the village and not given to extroversion. Don't get me wrong, they were great lads and I wasn't uncomfortable in their company. The lads and their girlfriends were associates of Elisabeth and therefore were alright as far as I was concerned. I spent half of that summer, all of autumn and winter and a bit of the following spring soaking up the atmosphere of a village much different to the one that I was raised in. I enjoyed it all thoroughly. My affection for the place has never left me although I have a mind that reciprocal feelings weren't always present amongst the inhabitants at the time. I joined the village football team and we played on The Eagle pitch up at the top of Delph Lane, roughly where Palinwood Road and Seven Acres now stand. The pitch sloped towards

Hull Mill Lane and a small stream ran through the middle of it when we had rain. In winter, bitterly cold winds howled across the pitch and must have been similar in temperature to those that try to flatten Antarctica. 'Enthusiastic' is the best way to describe the team's performance a lot of the time, although it had its moments playing in cup tournaments in the deep, dark reaches of the West Riding of Yorkshire. I don't recall winning trophies or medals. I think we won an argument with a referee one time, but you can't put that on your sideboard can you?

The village seems to be different now – maybe that's wrong, it's the people and their circumstances that have changed, and me of course.

25

Around the month of May or whenever Whitsuntide fell, I was introduced to the Saddleworth Brass Band Contest. The Whit Friday event ran in much lower key than it does today. It was mainly for the pleasure of the local people and the majority of band members were from the villages. The first contest I attended was in Delph and was held, as it is at this time of writing, outside the old Reform Club on Gartside Street. I suppose the event defined a traditional Yorkshire way of life or at least how it was thought to be; that of breezes blowing across moorland, woollen mills singing their desultory songs in the warm valleys, leek-growing and racing pigeons, although the latter two didn't apply in Saddleworth as far as I know.

Bands played their marching tunes as they trudged from coaches down to the playing venue. Most of the bands' uniforms seemed to be in various shades of plum with cap badges, epaulettes and buttons glistening in the sun. The odd band turned up decked out in pale, pastel colours, mainly blue. In a leafy village setting, on a warm summer evening, there is nothing better than listening to a good cornet player laying his notes onto eddying soft breezes, while you're paying attention to a glass of something cool and sparkling.

If one were fortunate and the contest was held on a sunny day, turnout was large and I often wondered where all the people came from. I think the woodwork that people supposedly pop out of must have been fairly extensive in some houses in the village – this being confirmed by the amount of empty glasses left on windowsills and doorsteps when the day was laid to rest.

Pubs were open early on Whit Friday and stayed open all day. Most of the bar staff looked a bit frazzled by early evening – some looked a sight worse than that. Quite a few topers came to the area from Oldham and surrounding districts. Speaking of out-of-town drinkers who wished to become comatose: they could often be found along with the indigenous folk lying behind walls with beer overflowing from their ears or telling good-natured policemen in Uppermill Square that they'd only had two gills and were just lying down, weary from sitting in the sun. The event saw very little trouble compared with the goings-on of recent years. It's been like an armed camp at times with mounted police and drink-to-clink police vans dashing about all over the place. It's calmed down a lot again, in the last 15 years.

It was a great day for the local kids, firing black peas at any human target that took their fancy. Elisabeth's younger brother and his best pal followed this pursuit with some enthusiasm and not a little imagination. Anyone standing still for too long became a target; black peas turned up in their ears, down shirtfronts, any pockets that didn't have hands in them and if they were very unlucky, their beer. By mid summer, some of the peas would have become growing plants, flourishing against walls and in cracks on the flagged side street pavements or cobbled frontages. Saddleworth pigeons were probably the best fed in England for a few days after the contests. I've seen them waddling along carrying their distended stomachs on little wheelbarrows – well maybe that's what they should have been doing, with their greatly distended crops and all.

Today there is much more of a carnival atmosphere. Every friend of a friend who's got a friend in Timbuktu turns up for the contests. On my return to the band contests after many years away, I could see that the event was being marketed as a business rather than a pleasurable occasion. Things change and not always for the better.

These days there are many more bands and venues. Some time ago someone from Dobcross began inviting bands from Bavaria and other European parts to participate in the contests. The contest is a great day out for all, although many band *aficionados* may not agree. At times there is difficulty hearing the bands play, because of alcohol-induced chattering. There are difficulties for local people trying to go about their business; the only place you are likely to be driving to in a hurry is 'Crackers'. On the many visits that I've made to the Church Fields, Dobcross venue, (we lived in the village for a number of years) I've noticed that the volume of speech rises when bands begin to play. Perhaps the organisers could find room for a Gas Band section during the period before the next band enters the contest arena.

I should add that I'm not a voice of authority when it comes to brass band music. Back in the early 'sixties, the likes of me didn't know his solo cornet from his Walls 99 ice cream wafer. I merely turn up as an observer to appreciate the efforts and find something to whinge about the day after. It helps to have a beer or two while I'm finding.

26

Saddleworth suffered a torrential downpour one late summer in the early nineteen 'sixties. Water formed a large lake near to the source of the River Tame at Denshaw, the containment was made by a blockage across a culvert situated on unused land between The Black Horse pub on Ripponden Road and the garden of a large house at the junction of Newhey Road and Ripponden Road. Water covered the garden of the house – which is built at road level with fairly extensive grounds – as well as flooding the upper valley. Apparently the blockage was caused by large pieces of debris getting jammed across the iron bars of the culvert, those having been fitted for that purpose. Wishing to do damage before it ran off down the valley, the gathering pool took a couple of aquatic vitamin pills and flexed its muscles. Under extreme pressure, the wall supporting the main road ruptured, water pushing the road and both footpaths into the valley on the opposite side of the road. With a great sucking whoop, the water set off down the valley as if it was late for its lunch.

The chasm that remained in the trunk road was some eight yards wide and below the road's normal base construction. Two days later amidst a lot of noisy trundling, umpteen efforts at measuring, some digging, plenty of hammering and after-lunch bellicosity (The Black Horse pub is in close proximity to the culvert), a Bailey Bridge was erected over the gap.

In Delph, three feet of water crossed King Street from Gartside Street, keeping pace with the greatly swollen river a few yards to its left and ran down the side of the chemist's shop towards Delph Band Club where it flooded the beer cellars – maybe the beer sellers too.

Trees came floating down in the torrent, lumps of wooden fencing, stuff from the allotments up by the riverside, a dustbin, someone's washing. It was powerful stuff and a lot of it got jammed under King Street's bridge. The row of houses named Brookside Terrace was flooded out with the sudden rise in the water level of the river, their frontages under a foot or so of water when the river was at its highest point. Later, when the cloudburst finished and the floods had subsided, we walked up to Swan Meadow and saw an old lady putting trout back into the river; unfortunately most of the stranded fish were dead.

27

I decided to acquire some form of transport rather than having to rely upon the inadequacies of the public transport system or the occasional lift home to Moorside from a mate. I couldn't afford to run a car even though I had a licence, so I made Soichiro Honda a little wealthier, and bought one of his motorbikes. My father, a motorcyclist for most of his life had provided me with a motorbike at the age of sixteen. I had to let it go after a year or so of falling off it. Alright that's not the real reason; it was because it spoiled my hairstyle, greatly interfering with my aspirations in the pursuit of girls. For most lads aged sixteen, girls have preference over motorbikes; the same premise probably applies to lads of sixty.

The other group of lads in the village were motorcyclists; they operated largely from Hardy's forecourt on King Street.

I will say at this point that for me there is nothing more exhilarating than riding a motorbike. Equally for your old chap in his Morris Minor, who has just been overtaken at twice the speed limit, there will be nothing more amusing than watching a fallen rider bouncing down the road on his backside in a shower of dust, flakes of paint and bits of expensive iron, issuing a volley of adjectives not to be found in most dictionaries. The incident has double the 'Whoops' factor if the motorbike is screaming its Japanese head off, asking for a mechanic's workshop long before it comes to a grinding halt.

The lads had most of the peculiarities that exist amongst the leather clad (on a parallel with those who are influenced by the changes in the moon). Business was conducted with plenty of swagger, a degree of surliness, many modes of dress, although there was a tendency for the brotherhood to be a bit tatty around the edges. There was also a leaning towards exaggeration when high speed was being discussed. High speed for those days was around 120mph, usually achieved just before the engine blew itself to kingdom come

A variety of machines made up the pack: Triumph Bonneville, B.S.A Gold Star, Velocette Viper, Ducati, Yamaha, a couple of

Hondas, an old Ariel and a big Norton visited periodically from Uppermill. To make the list a bit longer, a chap nicknamed The Flying Barman, rode his Francis Barnet motorbike through the village in the early evenings (his nickname suggests where he was bound). He negotiated the road-rise and quick-flick left outside the Bull's Head pub on King Street beautifully, raincoat tails and unbuckled belt flapping in the breeze. Propping up the vehicle list was the village bobby's Le Velocette, with its 200c.c. water-cooled engine. It was a lightweight, utilitarian machine and great for P.C. Dyson – he was a decent if formal bloke was Jack. The Velocette's performance was never going to worry the likes of the M.V. or Gilera racing outfits of the day. It probably wouldn't have worried a postman's pedal bike on a good day, if the postman were in a hurry.

Blissfully swishing along leafy country lanes is something that not many young motorcyclists enjoy, they are always in such a damn big hurry to get somewhere else. It was nice to drop out now and again and relax, especially on sunny, autumn days watching brown and yellow leaves leap into the air like roadside sorcerers scrambling awake, or seeing long grass bend rhythmically as if a bullfighter were drawing his cape over them. Who's to say that some wandering ghost wasn't keeping pace with you as gusts of wind tugged at your helmet or jacket? Sometimes when riding quickly uphill, clouds seemed to come rushing to meet you, or you might catch yourself watching colours changing hue in the distance as ridges and valleys unfurled before you. I often wondered if some Harley Davidson rider, on the long hot roads of an American Indian Summer, was grunting along at the same time as I. All life wasn't lived to the creed of speed. Now and again the roller blinds shot up revealing the world that everybody else lived in.

There is a price tag or scope for misinterpretation on anything that one enjoys as a youngster. If as a motorcyclist, you are a social sniffer, it's not safe to indulge your habit when being addressed by a police motorcyclist who's just pulled you in. Both you and he know that you've been speeding – the last time you looked at your bike's speedometer some miles back down the road, the speed limit was being exceeded by at least half of that permitted by law. Sniffing while the policeman is giving you a going over can be misconstrued as an act of disdain and encourage the officer to investigate your machine more thoroughly.

''Ere sonny, shouldn't you have brakes at both ends of the bike?' or 'Your back tyre must be drawing its pension because it's bald', or

'What's your road-fund licence holder doing with a beer mat in it?'

I was never guilty of those indiscretions, but they have happened to some.

Occasionally an outsider stopped off in the village and began banging on about how "quick" his motorbike was. Tony, the lad with the Triumph Bonneville, usually crushed such debate by cruising slowly into the village street and parking up alongside the boastful one. Were you of the opinion that you had a fast bike and wanted to put your theories into practice, the only thing you were likely to be theorising about was the empty space in front of you and the intoxicating smell of burnt engine oil as the 'Bonny' vanished over the horizon. When the Triumph Bonneville first arrived on the scene it was the fastest production bike that your average person could afford.

On occasion, when he was feeling happy, John Buck the lad with the Velocette Viper gave impromptu displays of how to swerve a bike in and out of cats-eyes in the middle of the road, sometimes at speed, often on wet road surfaces. These demonstrations occurred mainly outside the chemist's shop and the Co-operative Society premises on King Street. The pastime is not something I'd recommend unless you are an expert rider or you subscribe to a very good insurance company. If I remember correctly the Velocette was a touring bike when John acquired it. I don't know what sort of existence it had led in its life before John, but it was in for a rude awakening when it came to live in Delph. He stuck a fairing (windshield) on the bike, some clip-on handlebars, the bike probably never slept well from then on. John held the patent on craziness and was apt to do things that would make the average rider cringe. Throttle-happy as the days were long, he'd be wearing a big grin as he rode past wherever we were parked up. Amongst their many other attributes some riders are slightly off the wall as they say; John qualified for that distinction without exerting himself. His total disregard for the graveyard and its function in society was nothing short of bemusing. A chap with an undertaking business in the village often ran up onto King Street with his tape measure, upon hearing John and his motorbike approaching the village. He'd also be clutching a coffin brochure and had a hopeful look on his face. He hasn't got his hands on John yet; although they never give up in that business do they?

One sunny Sunday afternoon in King Street, Delph, there was a difference of opinion between two riders. The debate was about acceleration over a short distance. You know how it is; these things set off as banter, move on to facts and figures, become a debate, your ancestry becomes involved and before you could say 'Castrol R' they were sitting on their bikes, both toeing an imaginary line in the road, waiting for someone to shout 'Go'.

One of the contestants – another John – was as easy-going as they get and kept his bike in mint condition. At one time or another though John, like most of us, was an unpaid road sweeper. Slithering down the road, while not beneficial to ones backside, doesn't half boost trade for the motorcycle clothing industry. Tony, the Bonneville lad, once told me that he and his passenger also went slide-about on Oldham Road, Delph, removing a fair bit of skin from the palm of his passenger's hands. I recall losing a fair piece of skin from my thigh amid a shower of sparks, flying ice flakes and a host of unrepeatable words, as my bike took its leave of me at the top of Grains Road. After ice, oil slicks on the road are the biker's worst enemy. The trouble is, you can't see them.

Jack, the other competitor, owned a beautiful Gold Star (or 'Goldie' as it's known in leather town) one of the best examples I've ever seen; nice fairing, swept-back exhaust, racing seat and he kept it as shiny as a baptised forehead.

I watched the contest about to take place on the main street with some intrigue, not because I wished for any particular outcome to the event, mine was more of a parochial view, there was always the possibility that a third party might become involved, like a bus or a large lorry coming into the village from the opposite direction, which is Millgate. The point that I'm making is that it didn't take much to get some form of action up and running. If they tried to emulate that race now the whole kit and caboodle would probably expire in a flash of tangled metal, broken bones and solicitors' letters, the village being traffic-congested these days.

I saw Jack recently in The Royal Oak pub at Heights above Delph. My good lady Sylvia and I walked into the pub and saw Jack, who was stopping the bar from falling down while he was talking to Teddy, another lad from the village that I knew, so we joined them. I think that I only spoke three times. 'Hiya Ted' and 'Hiya Jack'; approximately one hour later as we were leaving 'See ya then'. Jack doesn't draw much breath once he starts talking; he is well travelled abroad and has a fund of biker tales when he settles down over a pint. As far as I know he is the only one still faithful to the bike and leather creed. Still, the sound emitted by a pack of modern-day motorbikes is like music to my ears, I try to locate the machines as they quicken away like devil riders, saddled on the wings of chance.

Ah, motorbikes! You've never lived until you've owned and regularly ridden one – a personal observation of course.

The 650cc Norton motorbike that I have mentioned previously came into my life one day, for something like ten minutes. The bike was quite big and scary, but it compensated for that by manufacturing adrenalin in ones body by the bucketful. Stuart its owner said I could give the bike a whirl so off we went in a huge cloud of ecstasy up Standedge Road to Castleshaw Camp Road. Had anything bigger than a mosquito been on the road on my 90 mph return past the Old Bell Inn, I would have been under a slab in the graveyard of Moorside Church. Considering that I've lived in the red zone for much of my life I should be dead by now – I haven't looked recently, maybe I am.

Here is a proverb that all bikers should take on board, "Never ride faster than your angel can fly".

28

Before the advent of radar, the "equipment" was a policeman in a fast car who could drive his vehicle quickly while keeping an eye on your speeding vehicle. He would have to be aware of any members of the public intent upon flinging themselves under his vehicle's wheels. He would also have to keep one eye on his companion who might be eating all the bacon sandwiches bought in the village butty shop. I've seen bobbies breakfasting al fresco (whilst driving); all those greasy crumbs must play hell with the uniform or at least the appearance of them. When radar speed traps first came into being, the police were underhand in their dealings with the motorist. What could look more innocent than a chap sitting in the rear window of a van, monitoring equipment, whilst writing out his shopping list or doing *The Times* crossword (Ho, Ho, as if...). In the first seven days of radar's introduction to Oldham, I contributed twice to the constabulary's Christmas Party. Making my way to the Honda Agents in Ashton, a pavement-mounted officer flagged me down. By the time I'd realised he was waving his clipboard in my direction I was passing the top of Bardsley Brew, which is roughly the boundary between Oldham and Ashton. Why would a policeman want to wave at me? I didn't know anyone in the constabulary at that time – so I went back to ask him. Without using big words he told me and gave me a piece of paper, filled with unintelligible claptrap, to commemorate the occasion. (Why do policemen always say 'thank you' when they're about to arrest your wallet?).

Magistrates are prone to bouts of ill feeling towards people who speed when in charge of anything with an internal combustion engine. I've never actually known a magistrate on a personal basis, although I have spoken to them from across a crowded room. Most of those conversations seemed to be about money and parting me from it.

You may recall that I had swapped some of my money for beer with the landlord of the Swan Inn earlier in these pages. That lack of judgement found me on Grains Road at night, a road that is not well illuminated even now. My motorbike had one of those headlights that lit everything for twenty yards on both sides of the road, but had all the penetrating power of a candle. Which meant that in my condition, dry-stone walls continually confronted me. My journey home took over an hour and was very much like trying to find your way out of a doorless room that isn't fitted with lights. Bikes and beer – bikes and burials more like!

This is where I came in with the dark night and the sliver of moon. I didn't surface in the village for quite a while after that last occurrence.

My younger sister Jean was doing a bit of courting with a lad from Shaw towards the end of my motorcycling days. The lad brought her home after they had been out on Saturday nights; it was the method for continuance for young men after they'd been on a date. Occasionally the lad missed the last bus home from Moorside into Oldham and the connection to Shaw. Our father or myself – when I arrived home – were in the draw for taking him home on our motorbikes when the bus was missed. If the weather was fine and father was feeling that way out, he would take him home. If not in either case, then that right became mine. Father was a slow steady rider; I was of the opposite persuasion. On the many occasions that we had rain, the lad would arrive home in a right state – this was before he learned about adverse weather and who provided his transport when that was so. Completing the rain-sodden journey he would dismount the bike and totter about the pavement until he'd got his nerves and his legs reasonably co-ordinated into something like their normal condition. With a weak-ish smile and some inaudible muttering he would express his thanks before wandering off into the night. His courting apparel was in second-hand condition most of the times I took him home. The lad showed a great deal of stoicism as fate cast him onto the winds of fear – he needed it by the bucketful to go out with our kid anyway. Those were some of the few occasions when our father and I could pass each other a knowing smirk as the lad and I prepared for take off. It's funny how someone else's discomfort has that effect on you.

29

If I may step out of the times for a short while, there was to be a lapse of ten years after motorbikes, before any constabulary wanted to interview me about speeding. It pains me to admit that I have been requested to remove a few zeros from our bank balance several times since those early days of entrapment. I haven't been discriminatory in choosing which police force I donate our money to either. I've helped to keep the civic authorities in a state of solvency in France, Italy, America three times and Canada twice (I'm a bloody slow learner). The Italian one doesn't really count; the machine-gun-carrying police sergeant, surrounded by his legions of lollipop-wavers in Florence said that I hadn't used the car's indicator when leaving a petrol station to join the flow of traffic. The moustachioed sergeant was a budding film star judging from his manner, which consisted in the main of staring into the distance and speaking to someone a yard away on my right-hand side, who wasn't actually present. The man was an excellent sniffer and his uniform didn't have a crumple anywhere. In the meanwhile, he kept his hands hooked into the machine-gun's neck strap. Between bouts of staccato barking he assumed a theatrically pained expression, as if he might be suffering from wind. He probably thought we were poor – even if we had the best and quickest Sierra that the Ford Motor Company produced at the time – I'm a bit scruffy when I'm out during the day. He walked around the car giving it a little pat here and there before muttering something out of the corner of his mouth to his senior plump lollipop-waver. The chap, wearing something similar to a bandsman's uniform wafted us on our way with a Clouseauesqe flourish. Lollipops are long slim white wooden batons with a grapefruit-sized orange disc on the end. Italian policemen like to wave them at you as you hurtle along, the presumption being that if contact is made and they are going to lose anything, it's the baton rather than their arm. I'm not condoning fast driving when I relate these matters; it's just how events happened. It's an afterthought at this end of my life, but speed is like a drug – once you get a liking for it, it never really leaves you, except under terminal circumstances of course. In those years when out buying a fresh car, usually one with a big thirst, I always headed for high performance cars powered by either Cosworth or Lotus engines. I've had my arm practically wrenched out of its socket at times before I would consider a more mundane type of vehicle. (Think of a screeching child in a shop, hanging on to a new bike, that it won't be owning in the foreseeable future).

Returning to the Italians, it's my contention that they don't understand their own language very well. I discovered that they had a deficiency in comprehension when Sylvia and I were driving to Gaeta, a small coastal town one hundred miles or so south of Rome. We entered Italy at Aosta on the Swiss border. Fuel in Switzerland was fairly expensive so we had decided to fill up with petrol once we had negotiated the Mont Blanc Tunnel. I should explain; petrol was very expensive in Italy prior to European countries becoming more integrated. In order to encourage motorists to visit the country, the Italian authorities ran a compensatory scheme in conjunction with the Automobile Association. It was possible to purchase a limited amount of fuel coupons from the A.A. allowing one to buy petrol (in Italy only) for something like half the normal price paid at the petrol pumps. I think the value of the coupons was £250 for which you paid £80, subsidising the cost in other words. I had no fear of communication with the people, having a basic knowledge of the language: Ferrari, Alfa Romeo, Autostrada, Carabinieri, plus being armed with a few expletives learned from a half-Italian bonehead from my past, known to me and our few mutual acquaintances as "Sep". He preferred Gus (Giuseppe) when he was sober – which wasn't very often. The man fancied himself as a fighter when really he was just a bad tempered punch-bag with more than his share of insecurities.

Waving my booklet of fuel coupons in the petrol attendant's face I said to him, 'You take-a da coupons, Si?' (Too many movies or what?) There were immediate gales of laughter from Sylvia who heard my performance through the open sunroof of our car – she laughed so much that eventually she got a stitch. The chap gave me a weary smile and replied in pretty good English that he did take fuel coupons. It was the same type of weary smile that an ice-cream vendor in Rome gave me later on in the holiday when I asked him for 'Due Gelato, per favor'.

He replied 'Larch or small?'

Because I wasn't listening properly to what he said, I thought he had said something in his mother tongue.

I repeated the request, this time holding up two fingers, 'No, Due, – two ice creams'.

He looked at me as if I'd just crawled out of a wine vat.

Slowly and resignedly he said, 'Two larch or two small ice cr-r-r-ims?'

We had to eat the ice creams before attempting to cross the roads; in Rome you're fair game for motorists if you're absent-mindedly absorbed in any way whatsoever. Many of the streets are one-way. Cars line up four or five abreast when traffic signals are against them; if caught immobile in the middle of a square or piazza you may have to face a row of snarling cars when the lights change. It's much like the feeling Christians must have had when standing amongst crouching carnivores in the Colosseum. As now, wiping the smile off the face of uppity foreigners was what it was all about. Local drivers looking for diversion sometimes see the colours on the traffic signals as simply a pleasant frame for the Vatican buildings in St. Peter's Square. When they decide to comply with a stop signal it's to the accompaniment of screeching tyres as their cars – most will have had a body readjustment – come to a furious halt. When they choose to ignore the red light – well, you'll all have been to a bowling alley.... .

For bemused onlookers there is nothing so entertaining or bladder-testingly amusing as a big-dealing Englishman caught adrift when the start gun fires. Or so Sylvia informs me, having spent much of that holiday with a bemused look on her face.

I take our cars into most cities on our travels, but not Rome, Florence or Naples if I can help it – the drivers in those cities are puddled. You're forgiven for thinking that there's a certain amount of irony in that statement.

30

Saturdays in Delph village were busy with shoppers going about their business until around lunchtime, say when Saturday morning workers returned home. After that, the village closed and you could doze off without fear of interruption. It was different on Sunday mornings. In mid to late summer, I would ride into the village and park up outside Hardy's shop in King Street at around ten o'clock in the morning. The place was as quiet as the rooms of a meditating monk. Smiling, the sun rose above Delph Hill, having chased the moon away towards the West with threats of dissolution. Streets in the deserted village lay cool and damp, particularly those that sunlight hadn't ferreted out yet. Steam rose in mirage-like curtains where heat from the sun warmed flaking stonework above the Swan Inn and the newspaper shop next door. Breezes whispered their way around the streets, drifting lazily amongst chimneystacks swirling the early smoke into dancing dervishes until they raced across the roofs, like Cossacks fleeing a battlefield. The three-road junction at the bottom of Stoneswood Road looked dew-dappled, dull and listless, a still-life watercolour painting that had lost its frame. Looking towards the White Lion pub, the grassed area on the curve of the road usually contained a few chickens or the odd guinea fowl, scratching about unconcernedly under the old black and white freestanding signpost. Positioned as it was near the edge of the road, the arms of the pole often took a swipe from a passing vehicle that had mounted the kerb while negotiating the bend. When that happened, the sign crookedly advised travellers that the road to Denshaw was through the side window of the White Lion pub. Rustling leaves in the trees of Delph Methodist Church garden sometimes broke the stillness. Singing softly, the river slid unconcernedly under King Street Bridge soothing the sun's hot temper before it was properly awake. Some mornings I'd walk up Delph Lane, where the wall of the White Lion pub seemed to be stroked by dappling shadows as the sun searched for a way through the churchyard's trees. The top of Delph Lane levels out and reveals the beautiful Castleshaw Valley unblemished at that time of day except for a tendril of smoke rising joyously from the roof of Castleshaw Camp School. A handful of buildings lay about the hillsides like scattered pebbles. If there was a light breeze, the uncut grass bowed as if an invisible giant was gently blowing on the meadows. The old disused church at Heights gazed out benignly over the surrounding hills, impotent now, where in its day it would have had respect, with its sun-blazed windows glinting like the eyes of a watchful eagle. The idea of Roman soldiers stamping across the forests or grasslands towards their fortress at the far end of the valley was pleasing. The idea of anyone that I might know, walking across the fields towards the camp, was equally so. Walking back down Standedge, past Delph and Dobcross Cricket Club, the cricket pitch lay low down like green baize except for the perfectly-manicured strip of wicket near to the middle. The sight gave me the impression that someone had splashed bleach in a long slim rectangle. It was easy to imagine the 1940s and the "plock" from a batsman striking the ball. Such genteel pastimes; he would be attired in white, baggy flannels and a shrunken woollen sleeveless cricket jersey; his white boots would have spikes in the sole and weigh three pounds apiece. Hair styles for the day were centre-parted and carefully flattened down with Brylcreem. No helmets or arm pads for them; the farthest thing from their minds was to try killing someone, as seems to be the case today. There was little to think about approaching The Old Bell Inn except that it had the looks and position of a staging post for weary travellers, in that case in its old livery it would have made a pretty picture for an artist to paint. If the Inn, when it was first built, wasn't sitting in solitary splendour alongside the old unmade road, it damn well ought to have been. A stone flagged floor under the old arch gave entrance to the yard at the rear and was worn as if many coaches had passed over it in its early days of usage. There have been all sorts of stories concerning the stay of past public figures – some even say that Royalty has sought refuge behind its walls. By the time I'd arrived back in the village, around noon say, a late-rising rider would sometimes be parked up alongside my bike. It was time for me to acknowledge the real world again.

Girlfriends came and went during my time amongst the green hills and cool valleys, some stayed longer than others but generally speaking, after the initial girl, I wasn't too bothered about anything long-term. Besides, the running costs of bike-ownership pretty well absorbed any spare cash that I had. On days when there was nothing better to do, we might all ride out to "The Ranch", a log cabin hangout for bikers at Crime Lake in Daisy Nook near Hollinwood. Other times it was Eades, a coffee shop on Union Street, Oldham and occasionally the Roxy Milk Bar at Hollinwood.

Pete and I went on holiday to Torquay a couple of times. On the first occasion we decided, early one Sunday morning, to go and take a look at Babbacombe. We were hammering down the short dual carriageway on the Torquay sea front on our bikes, singing hymns and reciting the Desiderata as you do, when a short person suddenly stepped off the kerb being pulled along by a small dog on its lead. I thought the person was a child at first and shouted at him the standard phrase prevalent amongst young men of that time, 'Please remove yourself from the highway, there's a good chappy'. The person did a quick skip out of the way, dragging the dog with him while shouting something unintelligible, but pointedly, to Pete, who was following immediately behind me. The small person was decidedly fortunate that his career hadn't come to a premature end right there and then. We must have missed hitting him only by a very small cat's whisker.

'We nearly rolled out Jimmy Clitheroe just then' said Pete as we pulled up at the end of the carriageway. Sure enough, we found out later that Jimmy was playing at one of the theatres along the seafront that summer.

The second time we visited the south coast we'd had trouble with Pete's bike before we set off on the journey. We decided that both of us would ride down on my bike, hanging any accoutrements that we could about our persons. A few days after reaching Torquay, the alternator on my Honda decided to pack up and the battery soon had no power. There were few Honda agents about in those days so the bike had to be shipped back on the train from Torquay, arriving at Clegg Street Station in Oldham five days from when I had last seen it. It would have been quicker to dismantle the blessed thing and send it home piece by piece through the post, or push it home.

Pete and I were heading for Blackpool one Sunday afternoon in mid-summer. It was a sunny day and traffic on the Preston bypass near Blackpool was very heavy – so heavy it was stopped. Motorways hadn't been built at that time. I don't know why I've said that, motorways are worse for getting blocked up than the old roads were. We pulled up behind a ragtop sports car with its hood down and were talking to each other, well we were shouting; it was a noisy little sod Pete's Ducati. One of our motorbikes, I forget which one, edged forward a few thousandths of an inch; in doing so it touched the rear bumper of the sports car. The car was very shiny where it was supposed to be and pale yellow in colour, but that was about the most you could say about it without being rude. Go on then, the car was a Triumph Spitfire. If you were to rip the top off an old Skoda you would get better performance from it than from a Spitfire. Well it wasn't exactly in the Ferrari or Aston Martin class, more of a boat on wheels that had lost its way. The bloke who was driving the car was a bit on the short side, one of those jersey-and-cords types. He sprang out of the car all of a lather and threw a little tantrum in the road on the offside of his car, jumping up and down as if his feet were on fire. He then made a very elaborate, nose to metal, job of inspecting the car's rear bumper. Having accomplished that, he started wearing out his shoes a little more before yelling something quite loud and rude with spit in it. It was one of those times when you can't help but laugh. I shouted to Pete, 'This bloke's a real clown, isn't he?'

Pete lifted his goggles onto his crash helmet, revealing a smirk on his face. The chap's neck swelled up at that and he looked as if he was going to burst something that he might need to carry on living. He seemed to make a concerted effort to rein-in those brain cells that weren't arming themselves and settled for relieving the pressure with another shouting do. Every time he used a swear word for emphasis the front of his hair lifted as if it were caught in a slight breeze. Eventually he got back into his car and slammed the door shut, five times as hard as the nudge that the bike had given it. By now all of the traffic in front of him had moved on about forty yards, he revved the poor little car's engine until its joints squeaked and the exhaust began to smoke alarmingly. With not much time left before either he or the car expired they trundled off to catch up with the queue down the road. It was difficult to assess whether the girl in the passenger seat of the car was impressed by his performance or not. We just pulled our bikes round the car when we caught up to it and went to the front of the line of traffic, smiling at the girl as we passed. The car driver's face was a lovely shade of puce by this time. I should think his ancestors were shaking out the welcome mat, just in case he decided to join them. People don't half get wound up about nothing.

Another first occurred for me when Pete and I were disturbing the pigeons at Shaw Hall, Greenfield, approaching Greenfield Station from the direction of the Farrar's Arms. Standing on the right-hand side of the road at the bus stop, just before the bends for the railway bridge, was what appeared to be a good-looking woman wearing a shortish, floral, overprinted frock. She had blonde curly hair and was shod with fairly high-heeled shoes. For obvious reasons there are no means of direct communication with your mate who is riding his machine some yards behind you. The prescribed method for showing your appreciation of a good looking woman or girl was to raise your right arm sideways with clenched fist, raising then lowering the fist, like a bodybuilder using a dumb-bell in one hand. Dumb-bell is appropriate in this instance. Having shown my appreciation in the prescribed manner we roared off towards Uppermill and from there to Delph.

Upon arrival in the village, Pete asked, 'Fancy that one at Greenfield Station did you?'

When I'd taken my crash hat off I said, 'Smart wasn't she, I could do her some good'.

Pete just smiled.

Suddenly my lambs-to-the-slaughter gene began jumping up and down and beeping in agitation.

I was somewhat puzzled by his attitude.

'Not bad if you like that kind of thing,' he said, leaving a few seconds free for any drama that might feel like showing itself.

'It was a bloke, ya know, thingymacallit, he's a cross-dresser', he said.

I'd always thought that cross-dressers were people who struggle to do up their buttons and fiddly bits.

I remember formulating a sentence, which was long and had a fairly descriptive line of expletives, beginning with 'Bloody' and ending with 'on toast'. I said it more than once – well, something similar to that the second time. Pete was decidedly chuffed about my mistake and told anyone who cared to listen about the incident. People are very interested when clever know-it-alls like me fall into the big-mistake pit.

The fall-out from that episode was that in the future, any female that I wished to accost or who might have had intentions of molesting me, had to undergo a surreptitious inspection for signs of beard stubble and chest hair before anything could be exchanged between us.

Towards the end of my time in the villages I was attracted to and by a woman who was not officially in the market because of some vows she'd made to someone else in church. The first time we met, as we passed on the bridge in the village, perhaps a year or so before the liaison, the girl, accompanied by her man of the time openly asked Elisabeth a couple of subtle questions.

'Who's this then?' and 'Can I have him when you've done with him?'

Flattery massages ones sense of importance and sometimes induces one to do a little public preening or smiling in self-satisfaction. On this occasion I had a feeling that if I responded to her overtures in any, way, shape or form, the temperature around Elisabeth would become sub-polar. Coughing discreetly in the general direction of Outer Mongolia, I hoped that it wasn't my destiny to be sent there if things took a change for the worse. Considering that it was such a sleepy little place, Saddleworth was beginning to look a bit like shark territory. I already had a beautiful girl and no ambitions to start a harem. I couldn't afford one anyway; there was a dearth of goats and camels amongst my items for barter.

This time, the lady and I met up at a party and it all went downhill from there.

My motorbike was pretty well known and it was still parked on a quiet lane at the rear of her house the next day. I was soon in trouble – my favourite place. The following morning the postman, milkman, local policeman, newspaper boy, half a dozen school children and the man who exercised his dog each morning walked past it. One of them evidently thought the revelation was newsworthy and told someone else who bust a gut to broadcast the news. In a village you couldn't even think something without everyone finding out what your thoughts had been. Once the drums had beaten out the message, the proverbial roof fell in. Shotguns were primed, reward notices posted and my social life was reduced to that normally enjoyed by a leper. The founding fathers of Saddleworth built their parapets fairly low. Keeping ones head below them for a while required a certain amount of dexterity.

Ah well, what the hell! I've never claimed to be a saint. Besides, in this case the old 'It takes two to tango' adage must come into play somewhere along the line. It's akin to lighting a match, it bursts into flame but it's soon gone out. In this life we spend a lot of time digging holes for ourselves and don't always know when to stop, it's a good idea to leave the spade at home. I suppose some people tread the untroubled path, eat their allocation of food, sail the backwaters and then die. It hasn't worked out that way for me, at home or in distant places, good or bad, that's how it's always been. In fraught times I've danced with the devil in his crumbling halls and when fortune has smiled, sipped wine on the mountains at sunrise.

168

A couple of years ago, Sylvia and I, rather than go directly along the A62 past The Old Bell Inn towards West Yorkshire, decided to take a detour through Delph village in our car. We met a tank-transporter with a Second World War tank on board, in King Street at the bottom of Grains Road, Delph. The driver took some time off our lives while he set about trying to get his vehicle to negotiate the road-rise and bend outside the Bull's Head pub. Apparently they were both on their way to Uppermill for an American Forces Day celebration. The cab in his vehicle rang loud with colourful quotations as the vehicle bottomed-out on the rising road and became stuck. His text appeared to be quotations from a pre-second-world-war German political harangue, rising in volume and splash content as it gathered pace. Above the noise of the vehicle's engine, when the haranguer paused for breath, I heard what sounded to be loud thumping noises of the kind heard when a flat piece of metal is being forcefully smitten. Gear crunching and bellowing from the vehicle's engine further disturbed the ambience, followed by a silent cooling-off period from driver and vehicle. Jumping from his vehicle, the driver treated his sizeable and knowledgeable audience (pub patrons) to a few unlikely proverbs mixed generously with utterances you wouldn't expect from the lips of a vicar. None of it sounded like the script from the film "Yanks" that had been being filmed in and around the village of Dobcross – although the cameo had an American feel about it. The man ran around his truck like a bee-stung nudist, waving his arms about and achieving nothing. We decided to drive up Grains Road before I became too old to remember where I was supposed to be going.

Pete and I worked together for a while at Stonebottom Mill, Dobcross. Well, he worked and I didn't do much. He had plenty of money – I hadn't. I was to become a weaver of cloth as well as a weaver of dreams – I did a short stint working nights some time during the employment. I can't say I liked the job; it was particularly noisy and hot in summer. I think on reflection that I only produced enough tartan cloth to keep a Highland caber-tosser's modesty intact. Maybe I managed a few bagpipe covers as well. According to legend at the mill, an old frightener named Chamley haunted the single-storey weaving shed section of the building. Anyone living in the dwellings numbered 1–9 The Wharf, Wool Road, Dobcross, who finds themselves reading this and hears the odd groan or the chink of coins during the evening hours, it's only Old Chamley on the prowl. I understand that the man had been the mill-owner at one time or other and can't get out of the habit of wandering around the premises, even though he's long passed on.

To produce something useful, be it large or small, as an owner or with assistance from a workforce, must have been very fulfilling. It's probably still so today, if man's unrelenting quest for riches doesn't overtake the pleasure in achievement of course. Perhaps the poet W.B. Yeats encapsulates a cloth manufacturer's aims in this beautiful extract from one of his poems.

> *Had I the heaven's embroidered cloths,*
> *Enwrought with golden and silver light,*
> *The blue and the dim and the dark cloths*
> *Of night and light and the half-light...*
>
> *(He Wishes for the Cloths of Heaven).*

Amongst its multi-cultural workers on the night shift, Stonebottom Mill employed a Ukrainian worker named Wasil doing some supplementary task. He was bobbin-carrying or something like that and based on the first floor of the mill. Basil, as he was known, was a bit on the short side, wore a flat cap that looked lived-in and rolled his eyes as if the world was too much for him at times. He also rolled his own cigarettes; they were thin tubes of cigarette paper filled with fresh air, a few strands of tobacco and a lot of optimism about their ability to burn. He was a bit on the deaf side, which meant he would set off on many unnecessary journeys due to misinterpretation, misfortune, mishearing or mischief. He was given to bouts of anxiety when something small was thrown towards the far end of the otherwise silent room that he worked in. His distress was relieved in a number of ways – going downstairs for an early brew or looking about him apprehensively or suspiciously before picking up a long-handled sweeping brush. Occasionally he released a rapid stream of words in his mother tongue while glaring dangerously from beneath his cap.

'Bliddy noise is commin with bang bang', he told us at break time, demonstrating his feigned disinterest with a bugger-off gesture of his arm. Most of the time he was a happy chap and smiled a lot. If he hadn't seen you for a while he'd say 'What you?' (How are you?)

There was an old whistle and spit radio situated on the second floor of the mill and I often went upstairs around nine o'clock to listen to the Cassius Clay – Sonny Liston fights of the time. Basil would sit there listening as well, although an understanding of our language wasn't high on his list of accomplishments. I would say he had the same level of English comprehension as I had of the language of the Kalahari Bushman. When the fight was over he would ask, with a walk-away show of indifference, who had won the contest.

I met a lot of nice people during my time at the mill; they were very friendly although some nodded a lot more than is usual for polite conversation – a few of them were quite deaf.

Around this time my parents decided to up-sticks and leave Moorside. They moved house permanently to live near the south coast of England, taking my younger sister with them. A pretty girl who lived in Denshaw and I had become acquainted over a short period of time and I was able to move in with her and her parents, which was very generous of them considering that they didn't know me from Adam. They would have been better off with Adam as it turned out. The attachment ran a fairly steady course and was a pretty good one, but it spluttered to a stop after a while because of my roving eye and an inability to master the craft of deception properly. I've spoken before about the village grapevine – this was another instance of that in full swing – from then on I've always referred to that bothersome vehicle as The Gripevine. As those of you who buck the system will know, your ear is never the best thing to find yourself slung out on. It was to be a couple of years before I perfected the art of seamless transition in all of my dealings. From that day onwards, however, I was able to stroll comfortably outside the usual parameters of normal society. After the unceremonious ejection I moved in with a Great Aunt who lived near Hill Stores in Oldham.

31

Sometime later I turned up in Uppermill where I became re-acquainted with Stuart the lad who'd owned the 650cc Norton motorbike previously mentioned. We had occasionally biked around as a foursome with our various girlfriends of the time. He was of the good-natured easy-smiling variety until he came into contact with anything that used petrol as a means of sustenance and required a road fund licence. He was quite single-minded when those criteria were met, his mission being to get to the end of each piece of road with as much speed as his vehicle's engine would permit. By that time Stuart was the owner of an MG Midget, a small but very nippy sports car. He was in a class of his own when it came to unfettered enjoyment; the distribution of his wealth to fund his favourite pastimes seemed to have had little restriction. Living it up for today was the recognised way amongst the young of that era, whereas I wanted to live it up for today, possibly the following week, maybe even stretch that to a month. Some were not similarly inclined – as you will see later.

Stuart owned a dinghy, which he moored at Dovestones Reservoir. Following in the footsteps of Lord Nelson wasn't my idea of fun – particularly when you think of his eventual demise and all that 'Kiss me Hardy' stuff. I never saw the reservoir from its surface or indeed underneath it. On sunny beer-free Sundays we went to check and admire the boat; although it's more than likely that the journey was made to see if there were any skimpily-clothed yachtswomen hauling their keels or splicing their main-braces or whatever it is they do when there is an interested audience admiring them from the shore.

On windy days the water contained in the reservoir was choppy, with whitecaps rolling ashore and making the edges of the reservoir a bit frothy. Incidentally, I've long held the opinion that anything under a white cap is not good for me: American policemen, chefs whose food you've maligned, cricket umpires that you've roundly cursed, customs officers when the car boot has been full of contraband – members of the Ku Klux Klan?

Musically, we were in Procul Harem territory – *A Whiter Shade Of Pale* – which could easily have been called "Another Yard Of Ale" because they were in orbit, full of booze when they wrote the song. All the bodies were present but their brains were somewhere off in the Woolly Mammoth period, probably trying to work out if elephant steaks would be a suitable accompaniment to a plate full of chips. The song was one of the most widely broadcast of its time, even though the lyrics are meaningless.

The Hippie Movement was just getting up steam, with many fume-filled bodies setting a course for Avalon, although why ordinary mortals would think they'd be given access to the resting place of heroes I've no idea. Unless it was thought that Glastonbury was a jumping-off point for what was after all an ephemeral pleasure. Taking all of that into consideration I'm fairly convinced that most of the flower-freaks and "junkies" didn't make it to the next town never mind Avalon. I recall the story of a space traveller so stretched out by his habit that he tried to set his brain on fire, when he came round he was being treated for first degree burns to his feet.

The Beach Boys were steering the popular song-boat with classics such as *The Sloop John B* and other harmony-driven songs like *Barbara Ann* and *Help Me Rhonda*.

Since she put me down, I've been out doin' in my head.
I come in late at night, an' in the morning I just stay late in bed.
Well Rhonda you look so fine,
                    an' I know it wouldn't take much time.
For you to, help me Rhonda, help me gid her outta' my heart.
Help me Rhonda, Help Help me Rhonda, Help me Rhonda, Help...

Everywhere you turned Brian Wilson was inviting you to visit surf city with his sun-and-sand songs. Six pints of bitter, a bit of imagination and a good jukebox could transport you there just the same – it goes without saying that it saved on the airfares too.

Prior to these times I had no idea what went on anywhere in Saddleworth outside a two-mile radius of Delph village. Life in the village of Uppermill was alien to me, even though for a while I'd had a girlfriend who lived in Dobcross and was on the fringe of the activities which I'm about to describe. The village was the nerve (just the one) centre of Saddleworth from which the Urban District Council dispensed its duties. It had life support systems similar to those that the rest of the villages enjoyed, *i.e.* a Co-operative Society Store, Post

Office, police presence on Buckley Street, access to two railway stations – one at each end of the village – just beyond its boundaries, a petrol station-cum-garage, schools, mills to provide work, a chip shop and one public house per head of population – that's a fib, but there was plenty of choice, if drinking was what you did to pass the time. It even had a milk bar – cool or what?

Before I go further I should say that sleepy little villages don't always have sleepy little people living in them. Farmers didn't lean on gates chewing pieces of straw while ruminating on the milk yield of a cow or spend time trying to work out how much winter snow they were due if ducks were flying in circles above the 18th hole on Saddleworth Golf Course. Generally speaking, Saddleworth people knew the score, were less inhibited than town folk and of course they had the Yorkshire Ingredient. (Which, as those in the know will tell you, is a secret).

My motorbike had gone by this time and I was bereft of any form of transport other than a Corporation bus. The dishevelled clothing and great-unwashed look peculiar to motorcyclists of that era had been replaced some time ago and I was back in decent suits, clean shoes, and presented a shiny face to anyone who cared to look in my direction.

By that time I was of a worldly-wise disposition and carrying a metaphorical pain in the backside that took me some years to prise off – the latter isn't relevant here.

There was a drink and party culture prevailing at that time; the drink bit notwithstanding, most of the party element was available to Stuart. I have, with occasional periods of time off for various reasons (usually because it was unavailable) enjoyed a drink. Sometimes more than one, often more than four, but I have never achieved the gold-medal drinking standard that some of my occasional associates have. There have been times when my alter ego has sat opposite me in the pub, club or wherever the spirit of drink might be dancing and stared at me accusingly until I've put my drink down. Exhibitionism hasn't been my forte either when around drink; I like to seek the deeper shadows when the big horns start to sound off. The shame attached to a public retelling of the time you were caught swinging from someone's chandelier shouting 'Wheeee, there she goes again' or when you were found hugging someone's drinks cabinet promising to marry it the next time around, are things that I couldn't happily contemplate.

Among drinking venues popular at the time was the Junction Inn, Denshaw where live music was on offer if you weren't particular about quality. Various artistes or groups provided the music, the names of which I'd never heard before nor wanted to again. The main preoccupation there was removing beer from the landlord's barrels as fast as he could pump it – some things don't change with the times do they? The Cloggers Arms on Lee Street, Uppermill was a popular venue at any time, The Cross Keys pub at the top of Church Road, Uppermill was a now-and-again visit. Other, less popular pubs were the ones you found yourself drinking in when you weren't drinking in the others. The jump-off point for most nocturnal activity was usually the Milk Bar in Uppermill Square. Drinking and driving was the rule rather than the exception. (It was during the period when drink-driving laws were just appearing on the statute books and infringers were not as heavily punished as they are today).

The only way to get to most of those entertainment venues was by car. (Buses only appeared when bus companies thought the bus stops might be unoccupied). If private-vehicle insurers had known what their inebriated customers got up to whilst driving their vehicles, they would have had a collective seizure. Leaving the Junction Inn after a session was a bit like the start of the Le Mans 24-hour race with considerably more tyre screeching. Overtaking on some of those rides was life threatening; be that as it may, it was attempted on any stretch of road with more than two hundred yards of uninterrupted visibility. Cars jostled for position until the outskirts of Delph were achieved. From there onwards the vehicles ran nose to tail until the column arrived at Delph Station crossroads. I remember Stuart, in a burst of uncharacteristic exuberance, overtaking the queue of cars waiting at the crossroads, passing on the wrong side of the road-centre bollards and shooting straight across the junction without stopping. Even my speed-accustomed eyes popped a bit at that manoeuvre; it was like showing a red rag to a bull as far as the following cars were concerned. The cars hurtled along the road at in-hell-by-breakfast speed down Measurements Straight, towards the outskirts of Dobcross village. The street lights whizzed past us like tracer-rounds fired from an automatic assault weapon; the lamps looked like floating blobs of yellow plasma as they flew past leaving a sound similar to "woosh-plock, woosh-plock". My pilot pulled out of the race about two hundred yards or so from the last bend at Duckworth's Corner, Dobcross. The Steering Wheel Jazz Club in Greenfield, situated off Shawhall Bank Road, was the final venue of most nights out. Once I asked Stuart why he'd reduced the speed of the car on the way down there. He said that he thought the thing was becoming too dangerous and anyway the other car drivers had drunk too much beer (Stuart had an understated sense of humour, it was quite worrying at times).

What is disturbing about the time was that nobody gave a damn about safety. We were sitting in the open-top car, our brains hanging out, ties flying in the breeze, faces fixed in expressions similar to those of diners presented with grilled steak at a vegetarian convention. It makes me shudder to think about it these days, I can tell you. This isn't a case of glamorising what was obviously a dangerous pastime. Drink/driving was a fact of life. Some drivers were so soaked in alcohol that it was visibly oozing from their pores. It's likely that there are pickled livers still roaming around from that era, perhaps enough to fill a shelf in the delicatessen in Uppermill. You may be amused at the thought, but some of the things that I've seen pickled in jars for human consumption while swinging through life, would astonish a hyena. Traffic was minimal in those days; anyone out and about driving at that time was probably in the same intoxicated condition as we were. We could all have gone to Hell in a cloud of petrol fumes and alcohol. Suit and tie were the going-out uniform then, so we were dressed for the occasion should it happen.

The steward of the "Jazz Club" could be a bit coy when entry to his premises was requested at just after 10.30pm, but usually a quick head count and profit calculation stopped any further reluctance. His initial complaint, 'If you can't drink here before half past ten at night, don't expect to drink here after half past ten', was wasted breath. The uttering of the wisdom came as he was throwing the doors open and bidding us enter the premises.

Stuart told me about one occasion when the more robust element amongst them had gate-crashed the Saddleworth Tennis Club's annual do – held on the upper floor of the "Jazz Club". In the ensuing uproar there was an accident whereby our lad accidentally sprayed the dress of the steward's wife with a soda siphon left standing on the bar. There were some at the do who thought that the dousing wasn't accidental. You can imagine the debating and finger pointing in the scrimmage that resulted from the unwanted shower. Apparently the dust settled down and after a period of shoulder shrugging amongst the men and squeaks of pique from the ladies, normal service was resumed. The word "accidental" becomes a matter for contemplation when blame needs attaching to someone's sartorial wreckage.

The lady usually got her revenge on some of her less vigilant customers by offering them home-made potato pie at a reasonable price. If you're looking for a good companion to blend with the alcohol resting in the confines of your stomach then salty pie should not be it. I'm pretty sure that the potato pie on offer had more than enough of the stuff within its pastry covered walls. Taking in salt is an incentive to the body to drink more liquid. The brain, not working to its full capacity by this stage of the evening, often decides to be rebellious and sends its couriers to the stomach with the message 'the stuff you're digesting is unfriendly'.

The stomach gets agitated and instructs its lawyers to begin divorce proceedings from the food.

The solicitor for the food says 'The nutrition has been paid for; therefore it should remain in situ'.

The attorney for the stomach says, 'With the new evidence about to be brought before the court, our case will be proven'.

At this point the defendant makes a bid for freedom and emerges from its sanctuary in a hot, directionless, hurry.

The presiding judge declares the issue null and void(ed).

Witnesses in the vicinity of the case take their clothes to be cleaned the following Monday morning.

There were some rascally people about in those days, one of whom owned a Sunbeam Alpine sports car and was a lady killer with an excellent pedigree. Legend had it that the chap could sometimes be observed popping out of a large bedroom window at the rear of a pub in Denshaw. I can't imagine what he was up too unless he was wallpapering. He'd drop onto the pub's out-shed roof and then into the rear car park, scaring the life out of the pub's guard-dog in the process. It was the same dog that I've mentioned previously, the one frightening public toilet users, so there was a certain amount of payback for the dog in the lad's venturing. I'm sure those assignations wouldn't have had anything to do with the landlord's daughters; people didn't do that sort of thing in those days, well I didn't – enjoy the attentions of landlord's daughters I mean.

The MG Midget sports car was beyond reproach in its willingness to grant maximum speed and could be driven flat out most of the time. It had a low centre of gravity and fairly good brakes, which meant spending very little time in prayers to St. Christopher, although sometimes, an element of faith in the car's ability to stay on its feet under duress, crept into my mate's driving. That belief provided an extra dimension to most journeys because there was nothing between the top of your head and the road surface if there was a catastrophe. An instance of that faith occurred one sunny Sunday lunchtime. We were returning from the direction of Mossley – with two girls sitting on the back rim of the car's cockpit, (there being no hood on the car at the time) – and fast approaching the Farrars Arms pub on Oldham Road. I think we'd been to an all-night party somewhere in the village of Mossley, a couple of miles away. Lunchtime clientele were sitting outside "The Farrars" in the sunshine, enjoying glasses of jolly-juice and besporting themselves in a loud and time-honoured manner. Approaching the pub, Stuart changed to a lower gear and the car quickly accelerated, lifting up onto two wheels as it negotiated the slight bend in front of the pub, almost depositing the two girls amongst the seated drinkers. If they hadn't been before, the girls were fully awake and paying attention, albeit in a slightly flustered and confused state. God only knows what the drinking folk were thinking as their beer flew in all directions in their hurry to escape our possible landing amongst them. 'Ooo look Doris, he's going to bring that sports car up here onto the patio'.

We roared past the pub, with us on the nearside grazing our elbows on the footpath. When everyone, including the car, had regained a reasonable level of dignity and we humans had returned to breathing evenly, I said what I supposed the other two passengers were thinking.

'Didn't think we were going to make it that time mate'.

'Nah, it's not a problem for this car," Stuart shouted, as he tipped the car the other way rounding the second bend at the top of Greenfield Station brow. Everyone had to adjust themselves again before we headed for Uppermill – we didn't see the girls again, not on a personal level anyway. You've no idea how closely disaster stalked us in those days. I suppose that if one has no sensible standard to work from, then one does what everyone else does at the time. Anyway, after all that devil-baiting, Stuart is still around, although I should think that the MG was made into razor blades and barbed wire many years ago.

A further instance of drinkers' disregard for personal safety occurred as two chaps who lived in my home village of Moorside, went drinking in the Bull's Head at Grains Bar one night. They were returning home, partially marinated, in a car owned by one of them, when the vehicle left the road on the quarry bend at Grains Bar. The car careered behind a large advertisement hoarding and down the steep hill of the meadow until a wall stepped up to prevent it going any further. The men weren't found until later on the next day, their bodies cold as turkey on Boxing Day.

I'm not without fault in that department, although to a much lesser extent. I once owned a second-hand, navy-blue Ford Cortina, Mark One and managed to get the car onto its roof at a crossroads in Elland or Brighouse, West Yorkshire late one Sunday night. I was returning home from Durham, having spent the weekend up there with my girlfriend of the time, who was at college on the outskirts of the city. Tiredness, misty drizzle and an invisible Stop sign (hiding behind a leafy tree) were my reasons given when an attendant policeman asked me, in the best room of a pub at the scene, 'What the hell were you doing to get the car on its roof?'

You can bet your next year's wages that the two pints of beer, consumed in a hostelry before leaving Durham, didn't help much. Medium-sized cars in those days weren't sprung for the speed they were sometimes asked to produce. The accident occurred when I realised there was a road junction immediately ahead of me and spun the steering wheel while stamping on the brakes, the car just flipped over. No one else involved, no bruises, just me hanging upside down wondering where the streetlights had gone. Some men ran out of a pub and helped me right the car – there is always a pub nearby when I have a misjudgement – the upper part of the car was tilted to one side towards the kerb. No broken windows, but a one inch gap between roof and driver's door meant a damp journey home, some three quarters of an hour later. The car went off to be made into dustbins, tooth fillings or settee castors, wherever dead cars go to qualify for resurgence.

The magistrates at Brighouse seemed to be impressed with my explanation, even smiled a lot at my explanation, they still removed some money from my pocket and stamped my driving passport. My licence over a three-year period had more spots on it than a window in a downpour.

32

A recently-retired pillar (one of those pillars that used to prop up the law enforcement building on Buckley Street, Uppermill) of the Saddleworth community, wasn't averse to investment in the cause of youthful celebration in those days. There was an occasion that I remember well, involving our pillar, his Land Rover and the best part of a pint of beer. After a lot of arguing with the steward and his wife, who wanted to close the doors, our noisy band of wisdom-bereft revellers was taking its leave of the Greenfield Jazz Club in the early hours of Monday morning. The Land Rover in question was waiting patiently in the car park, its engine purring contentedly, while the recently-retired was seated inside the vehicle deep in conversation with a pedestrian who seemed, in turn, to be in deep conversation with his own foot. A few of us clustered around, as you do when wisdom is about to leave the scene and that deity of mischief makers "Shuddaknownbetter" was taking a firm grip on proceedings. Conversation with the pedestrian was proving difficult because he kept sliding down the Land Rover's door and reappearing outside the window before sliding down again. Eventually he found a leg that would support him and the conversation was maintained unbroken, if not coherently. The conversation was about the technical ability and driving skill required for the beer glass and contents to stay balanced on the Land Rover's bonnet while the driver negotiated the route along Shaw Hall Bank Road, up Oaklands Road, along Oldham Road to Greenfield Station, down Station Brew and back to the "Jazz Club" with the beer mug and contents still in place. The conversation was threaded through with 'Albetcha's' and 'Course ah cans'. Even I, who had been present at some pretty unlikely scenes where sanity had run off over a hill, wasn't buying that one. You may scoff at the likelihood of the objective being achieved, but I can tell you that the vehicle and its point of interest managed to leave the premises and set off along Shaw Hall Bank Road, with its load still balanced determinedly on the bonnet. We realised some fifteen minutes later however, that the ensemble or even part of it wasn't about to return in the immediate future. Two possibilities occurred to me – perhaps a couple of days later. The first, that the driver jumped out of the vehicle when safely out of range and drank the glass of beer. Second and much more likely, was that the pot and its contents met their demise quite early on in their journey and the driver had said something like "Sod this for a tale" and cleared off home to bed. Martin, the recently retired, was a very nice chap – he still is.

Finding ourselves without a place to drink, late one evening (because the "Jazz Club" steward was working himself up into a seizure about something or other – in a burst of self-important peevishness he wouldn't let us onto the premises) Stuart remembered that there was an all-night send-off party in Delph. The party, when we eventually found it, was disturbing the tranquillity surrounding an old stone property situated just before Hull Mill Lane towards the far end of Delph Lane. I know not who the party-giver was or where she was being sent to. We arrived just before midnight when the party spirit seemed intent on lifting the roof of the building a few inches higher than the building had planning permission for. The place was bursting at the seams with people. There was enough beer in the kitchen to float a riverboat and the music was doing its best to shatter any fine glassware unlucky enough to be within a few yards of the music's source. Stuart found the host and they held one of those conversations where one person hasn't a clue what the other person is talking about, the type that consists of nods when a headshake is required. After a reasonable amount of bellowing in the direction of the hostess's ear and a few shoulder shrugs from her, we were pointed in the direction of the pile of booze and the lady wandered off. I never saw her again and wouldn't be able to tell who she was if she hit me on the head with one of her Trini Lopez records.   Although he was absent from the party, Trini Lopez spent all the late evening telling everyone what he would do if he had a hammer.

If I had been in charge of a hammer, the communication from Mr. Lopez would have been in big trouble, if I'd been able to locate the source of course. Somebody had lifted the armature of the record player and not returned it to its proper position; consequently the same record kept playing. There were extension speakers all over the place in the room but there was no sign of a record player. Anyway, attempts to root out the music machine were seriously impaired by a rather large lady who bounced around to the music, tapping down any loose nails in the floorboards, making the resident goldfish nervous and generally getting in the way of everyone.

Her companion, a quiet-looking individual, was sitting in a deep armchair holding a bottle of beer in one hand and a glass in the other. He had the look of a man who'd just seen his wallet fall into an industrial shredder. His arms were stretched out in front of him, resting on the sides of the chair. Whether he was ready to deflect the large lady should she fling herself upon him in a fit of passion or should she accidentally fall on him in the middle of some intricate dance routine, is a matter for conjecture. The Trini Lopez song and the large lady were a damn nuisance for most of the rest of the evening. Recording artists have no idea of the problems they cause, having once committed their voices to some form of plastic.

In the course of eating, drinking and talking, these dos move along quickly and before I knew it, the sun was rising over Harrop Edge – the hillside separating Delph from Diggle.

In those years, Diggle village consisted of a few rows of terraced stone houses, a small, council-owned housing estate, school, church, the denomination of which I never knew, with a scattering of cottages and farms about the hillsides. The Hanging Gate pub, the Diggle Hotel and Diggle Band Club provided entertainment. Dobcross Loomworks (now Shaw's Pallets) and Warth Mill provided work. A few mixed shops and the Post Office catered to local needs. It had its own railway station, but I wouldn't be certain where it was situated. Diggle was a place usually passed through at a fair rate of knots.

Stepping outside from the party, the air was fresh and clean and there was no identifiable noise with the door closed. I ambled back inside to look for Stuart, stopping on the way to appraise myself in the hallway mirror. I remember thinking that my face looked as if it had been pulled around until it looked like a lump of old putty lying on a joiner's bench. Someone must have found the record player just as we were finally about to leave the premises. Richie Valens started singing *La bamba* and the large lady set about driving the floorboard nails home with a vengeance. The house seemed to have survived the onslaught from the good lady, without subsidence or loss of mortar from the masonry, the next time I passed it.

Amongst its many other virtues, the MG Midget, was a good little car for wiping away those cobwebs that had gathered during the night's diversions, burbling along the roads quietly as if aware of our delicate condition. Cold, early morning air is a good face straightener for those who wear their heads back to front first thing in the morning. My Great Aunt was most surprised as I walked in with the milk at 6.30a.m., after Stuart had dropped me off outside her home.

Eventually Stuart packed his trunk and abandoned ship, going to live in South Africa.

I for my sins and with help from the supreme deity spent the next few years trying to resist the powerful pull of the graveyard.

33

When I had first stepped over the Yorkshire border at Grains Bar as a youngster (the one permitting entry into Saddleworth) – and closed the gate afterwards of course – I thought that I was entering a place directly in line with my need for reserve and genteel sophistication. To some extent that ideal was met, the world moved a lot more slowly then and older people generally were of the amiable variety – the only individuals likely to be fractious were those of my generation. In fact some of them were so amiable they had ambled off into the Old Wild West. Saddleworth has given shelter to a few frustrated cowboys in its time. I almost fell off my motorbike in amazement at my first close sighting of the rare breed, at Delph Station crossroads one day. The chap was standing on the corner of Huddersfield Road and The Sound with arms folded, squinting into the midday heat from under his wide-brimmed Stetson. The rest of his ensemble comprised a cowboy shirt, Levis, neckerchief and boots. He looked as if he was waiting for the next stagecoach to Huddersfield. Apparently he lived nearby and could often be seen guarding the southern entry to the village. I would have liked to have been around the area if a car or motorbike engine had slipped out of timing and backfired – a common occurrence in those days. I bet the cool dude would have become a bit anxious, wondering who was taking pot shots at him.

At this point I should introduce Winston, an old friend, (more old than friend, ho, ho!) workmate and best man at my wedding, who has inclinations along the trail normally ridden by the likes of John Wayne and Clint Eastwood. He likes all stuff "Western" including Country Music, which he sings a little off key and rather loudly. He is seriously attentive when he sees anything edible or wearable that comes from a cow and "jest-lurves" Cherokee Jeeps. He must have a secret oil well somewhere because the latter only do the same amount of miles per gallon as the ceiling of numeracy present in my wife's youngest grandson – he's sticking at around twelve at this time of writing. Winston and I were two of six inspectors all sharing the same office at our place of employment. Amongst his finer attributes the man has a firm grip on the knowledge and application of basic mathematics. This I know from an experience that occurred one time when Sylvia and I took a fortnight's holiday somewhere out of the country. I had been in the habit of keeping a salt cellar full of reduced-sodium salt in my desk drawer in case I ate in the office at lunchtime. Winston was inclined to use the condiment occasionally – particularly when I wasn't present. Upon returning from our holiday I found that the salt cellar was empty. When I asked Winston what had happened to the salt – had he been practising a bit of pre-season gritting or some pelt curing, he said, 'I had to use twice as much salt on my sandwiches because the salt's low sodium – i'n't it?' There isn't anywhere you can go after that, I suppose.

In those days, at various times, the clump, clump of cowboy boots could be heard stomping their way around the district, adding a peculiar tone to the otherwise undisturbed tranquility of the place. Ah, the trail between Dobcross and Delph was littered with prairie-dog holes and scalp-hunters. I suppose that the holes situation hasn't changed much since then. Come to think of it, someone must have put a name to the pile of rocks on the heights above Chew Valley. The recumbent Indian's Head could easily have been called something with a more local theme like Shepherd's Brow or Weaver's Peak.

Passing through Saddleworth today it's hard to imagine a time when the streets were empty after six pm. Pubs were dark, austere places and frequented by just a few taproom regulars during the week. The work ethic was paramount and manufacturing was predominately textiles. Everything was as natural as the Lord intended, many side roads were unmade, fields abounded with hedgerows, traffic flow was desultory at best and nothing on the landscape had been sculpted, like Churchill Playing Fields or Saddleworth Golf Club. Still, I suppose you can only live in your time and wonder about the past with a little help from the likes of me.

The friends and associates mentioned in the book, without exception, are happy to have done a return journey to our past and we've spent an hour or two chewing it over. As for going back to those days – I don't think so. It would be too great a pull to give up the new Mercedes, big 'V'4 Honda motorbikes, globetrotting holidays and detached, many-bedroomed, properties that are a part of their lives these days.

THE WHITE LION – DELPH

Full, the yellow moon is on the rise above Knott Hill.
Soundly sleeps the village under silver roofs, until
Slouching, dark and sullen, by the graveyard on the bend,
The graveyard where its dwellers have arisen to attend,
The Lion holds a gathering and the dwellers have a gill.

Strikes the old church clock, at a quarter after three
Turns the landlord often, restless sleep for him will be.
Silent through the village drives a coach and to the rear,
In all their pomp and splendour, rides a troop of cavalier,
To dismount with a flourish, by the ageing chestnut tree.

Gently turns the landlord in his undisturbed repose.
From sleek and lacquered carriages, step maids in satin clothes.
On thoroughbreds come gentry, in silks and finery
In the silence of that silver night no better sight could be.
They walked in through the oaken door, though it was firmly closed.

Long the talk of chivalry and sweet the maidens' laughter.
With ale and gentle ribaldry, the cavalry were after
A lady, slim with raven hair and deep her tawny eyes.
In white the youngest cavalier and not yet worldly wise
Kissed the one of raven hair, though what befall thereafter.

Quiet the husband's challenge and swiftly strikes the sword.
Bold, the cavalier, had received his last reward.
Still, the feckless soldier lay, upon the stony floor.
His hat had gone a-spinning down the passage to the door
And silently its feather settled of its own accord.

Silence for the soldier, so lifeless and so white.
Remembered deeds of battle this lion of the fight.
So gently came the weeping and softly chimed the bell
For one and all the leaving and the dead youth carried well
Through the door closed firmly they walked into the night.

Early in the morning, with breakfasting all done
The landlord and his lady, their day's work just begun.
How odd, half empty barrels and stains across the floor,
All the signs of revelry, though firmly closed the door.
And there, an ostrich feather rocking gently in the sun.

David. J. Lavisher   1995.